THE
ONE HOUR
GARDEN

THE ONE HOUR GARDEN

Laurence Fleming

With Plans and Line Drawings
by the Author
and 16 Colour Plates

WARD LOCK

To
JANE

First published in Great Britain in 1985
by Ward Lock Limited, Villiers House 41-47 Strand.
London WC2N 5JE

Reissued 1993
© Studley Ltd 1985

This book was designed and produced for the publisher
by Antler Books Ltd, 11 Rathbone Place, London W1P 1DE

Text set by Falcon Graphic Art Ltd

Printed in Italy

British Library Cataloguing in Publication Data

Fleming, Laurence
The one hour garden
1. Gardening
I. Title
635   SB450.97

ISBN 1-85079-224-0

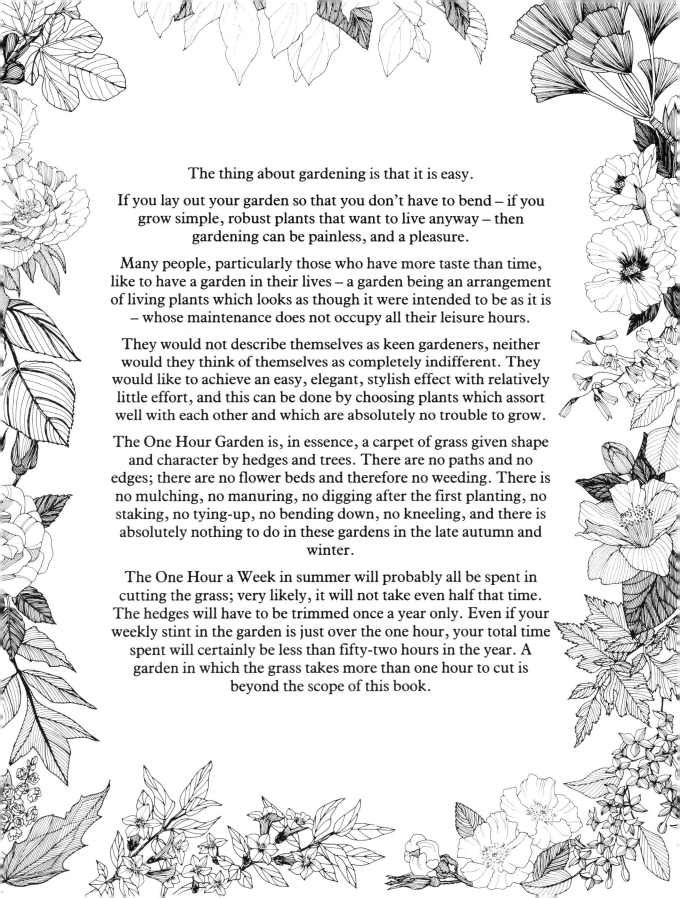

The thing about gardening is that it is easy.

If you lay out your garden so that you don't have to bend – if you grow simple, robust plants that want to live anyway – then gardening can be painless, and a pleasure.

Many people, particularly those who have more taste than time, like to have a garden in their lives – a garden being an arrangement of living plants which looks as though it were intended to be as it is – whose maintenance does not occupy all their leisure hours.

They would not describe themselves as keen gardeners, neither would they think of themselves as completely indifferent. They would like to achieve an easy, elegant, stylish effect with relatively little effort, and this can be done by choosing plants which assort well with each other and which are absolutely no trouble to grow.

The One Hour Garden is, in essence, a carpet of grass given shape and character by hedges and trees. There are no paths and no edges; there are no flower beds and therefore no weeding. There is no mulching, no manuring, no digging after the first planting, no staking, no tying-up, no bending down, no kneeling, and there is absolutely nothing to do in these gardens in the late autumn and winter.

The One Hour a Week in summer will probably all be spent in cutting the grass; very likely, it will not take even half that time. The hedges will have to be trimmed once a year only. Even if your weekly stint in the garden is just over the one hour, your total time spent will certainly be less than fifty-two hours in the year. A garden in which the grass takes more than one hour to cut is beyond the scope of this book.

THE ABSOLUTE MINIMUM GARDEN

This garden consists of hedges round three sides of a rectangle of grass, the house making the fourth side (figure 1). It is larger, but not much, than fifteen feet square (4.50 m.); smaller than that it is a Front, or Back, Yard and is treated later in this book.

If there is a tree already there, either grass up to it, leaving a little space between it and the grass to let it breathe, or else pave up to it, again leaving it room to expand. If the tree is against the wall, or fence, then include it in your hedge, planting its neighbouring shrubs at least three feet (90 cm.) away from it.

If your Absolute Minimum faces the north, or is much overshadowed by your neighbours' trees, then it should be paved. Grass must have sunshine in order to grow well. It does, however, make a garden look more like a garden than paving. Paving is expensive, can be hot and uncomfortable in the summer and sullen and slippery in the winter. It is advisable only in small, dark gardens more accustomed to being looked at than walked in.

To maintain this garden, you will need a pair of garden shears to trim the hedges and a push mower to cut the grass. A stiff broom is a good idea, either to sweep the 'lawn' or the paving. The grass clippings can be laid round the young shrubs to keep the weeds down and, in this case, they should be 'forked over' in early autumn. For this a handfork will do – on this scale – using a sort of rotary wrist action. You will need a spade to plant your shrubs but, as this will be the sole planting in your garden, you can probably borrow it.

Figure 1
Plan of an Absolute Minimum
Garden, very dark and overshadowed by other people's
trees. Hedges of different
shade-bearing shrubs round
three sides give an appearance
of order. The space between is
paved as it would be too dark
for grass.

THE MINIMUM GARDEN

This is slightly larger than the Absolute Minimum, perhaps eighteen feet wide (5.40 m.) and forty feet long (12 m.). Again, hedges are planted round three sides, but there is room now for a transverse hedge, across the garden making the end of the garden into a square (figure 2): that is to say, if your garden is eighteen feet wide (5.40 m.) your hedge is planted eighteen feet (5.40 m.) from the end of the garden.

If you have no long measure, take a piece of string, or rope, and make it the same length as the width of the garden. Then put one end at the end of the garden and plant your hedge at the other end. A hedge, in this context, is a row of the same shrub planted at, let us say, three foot (90 cm.) intervals so that they join up and can be clipped flat at the front and on top. The hedges suggested for these small gardens (on page 14 and page 15) should need clipping only once a year, in late summer, the end of July or early August in England.

A push mower should still be adequate for this garden; many motor mowers of my acquaintance take, in any case, more than an hour to get started.

Grass seed can be sown in March or September, on well-prepared, stone-free soil. Turf can be laid at almost any time, provided it can be generously watered, either by you or the heavens, every day until it 'knits', probably a fortnight or three weeks, rather depending on the time of year. If it does dry out and curl up at the edges it never really comes right. Therefore, do not lay your turf and go away on holiday.

Grass has been the basis of the English Garden since the Middle Ages and it is really the best foundation for the Minimum Garden.

If hedges are to be the sole ornament of your garden, then they are better to be evergreen, that is to say to keep their leaves during the winter.

You can 'clip tight', creating a solid wall of leaves, with a firm, flat top and sharp corners. This gives a smart, architectural effect suitable in small, or narrow, gardens but it is only successful with small-leaved shrubs whose flowers are entirely unimportant.

9

Figure 2
Plan of a Minimum Garden. A hedge of Griselinia littoralis in front of the right-hand wall and one of Pyracantha across the top. Against the north-facing wall on the left – Elaeagnus ebingii at the top, Euonymus japonica at the bottom. Escallonia makes the transverse hedge.

Figure 4
Plan of a Minimum Garden. The two strips of paving make the central section of the garden into a square. At the right, a hedge of Escallonia, at the left one of Pyracantha, both to be clipped loose. The Choisya at the top could be grown free.

Figure 3
Plan of a Minimum Garden. A hedge of Choisya across the top, with one of Pyracantha half way down and one of Viburnum tinus at the bottom. These hedges are equidistant (See illustration on page 12).

You can 'clip loose' – that is to say, give your hedges the freedom to flower, cutting them back only very gently with secateurs, so that the front surface is even but not perfectly vertical and the top is neat but not perfectly flat. Secateurs are a kind of strong garden scissors and it is well worth buying really good ones.

Or your shrubs can 'grow free' – wise only if you have plenty of room. The shrubs are cut back only if they begin to get too large. For the Minimum Garden, loose clipping is probably the most satisfactory, but at figures 3 and 4 are plans for a Minimum Garden where the shrubs could also be grown free.

By having a different kind of hedge on each side of the garden – light green, bright green and dark green – a simple, almost dramatic, effect is very easily achieved. You will have to choose only three kinds of shrub for the Absolute Minimum, but if your garden is long and thin then you can cut it across with a fourth hedge, leaving room to get round one end, *not* in the middle (figure 2). Two short hedges on either side of the way through would merely emphasise the narrowness of the garden.

The hedges should be planted between October and March (or between March and October in the southern hemisphere), although there are those who recommend evergreen planting in September and in May. The ground should be well dug to a depth of at least 18 inches (45 cm.), and generously manured. The beds should be eighteen inches (45 cm.) wide. It will take some time for the shrubs to meet and during this time there will be some weeding to be done, most conveniently with a hoe. A hoe is a thin iron blade fixed transversely at the end of a long handle. Covering the earth between the shrubs with grass clippings is a good way of keeping the weeds down. Once the hedges are complete, however, there will be few weeds, particularly if the grass is allowed to grow right up to them, and maintenance on them will consist only of the once-a-year haircut.

Hedges for the Minimum Garden
Almost any shrub can be clipped into a hedge, but we are here

concerned with those that are easy to grow, in any aspect and in any soil, and – above all – which are not so vigorous that they have to be clipped more than once a year.

Many of the best evergreen shrubs for this purpose have no English name, being found in foreign parts by foreign botanists who named them after themselves or some other admired person. The Latin names are therefore, unfortunately, unavoidable, and they are also essential when buying plants as, without the precise botanical name, you may get something you absolutely do not want.

The Mexican Orange (Choisya ternata) is a generous, accommodating shrub with deeply cut, bright green shiny leaves and scented white flowers in early summer and frequently later. It will grow in shade, although it may not flower there, but would be at risk facing the north. It must be sheltered – either by the house or a wall, or a solid fence – as it detests wind. At its best grown free, facing the sun.

A Minimum Garden. A hedge of Escallonia, with one of Elaeagnus ebingii (left) and one of Euonymus japonica (right) on either side, cuts across the garden, with a hedge of Griselinia littoralis beyond it. On the left, the end wall is covered with Pyracantha. The trees are in the next door garden.

A Minimum Garden in
December. In the foreground,
a hedge of Viburnum tinus is in
bloom; in the middle, the
Pyracantha is covered with
berries; at the end there are still
a few last flowers on the
Choisya (see figure 3).

Laurustinus (Viburnum tinus), from south-eastern Europe, has a satiny, very dark green leaf and heads of small white flowers in the late autumn and throughout the winter, sometimes later depending on its position. It is strong and hardy and will grow facing north, though it probably will not flower. Clip loose.

Griselinia littoralis (of the coast) comes from New Zealand and is certainly happier within ten miles (16 km.) of the sea. It has beautiful apple-green leaves, slightly shiny, ending in a sort of rounded point. It is better with a fence or wall behind it, prefers to face the sun, and likes quite a lot of water. Clip loose.

Euonymus japonica has very brilliant glossy leaves and a greenish, whitish bunch of flowers in the summer. Like many other Japanese shrubs, it will grow in the most inhospitable places, but nevertheless responds well to kindness. Clip loose.

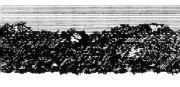

Eleagnus ebingii is a handsome, vigorous hybrid with Japanese parents, not occurring in Nature. Its mature leaves are of an unusual shade of greyish green, matt and soothing to look at. Tiny white flowers when grown free, but would be better clipped loose in the Minimum Garden.

The Firethorn (Pyracantha), originally from Southern Europe, has many varieties, all of which make excellent hedges. It is better clipped loose, will grow facing north or in shade, has bunches of creamy-white flowers in early summer, followed by spectacular red, yellow or orange berries – depending on which variety you choose – which frequently last through the winter. It does, however, have thorns which, while they will not prick you as you brush past, make it an uncomfortable shrub to fall into. It has small leaves of a middling green and *can* be clipped tight, if you start when it is young and are prepared to forego the berries.

The Escallonias, from South America, are particularly beautiful small-leaved evergreens, with white, pale or deep pink flowers. They prefer some sun and like water – being especially at home in the West of Scotland – and they are much hardier than they look. Clip loose or grow free, depending on the variety – some have much larger leaves than others. They can also be clipped tight and, amazingly, continue to flower *within* the resulting hedge.

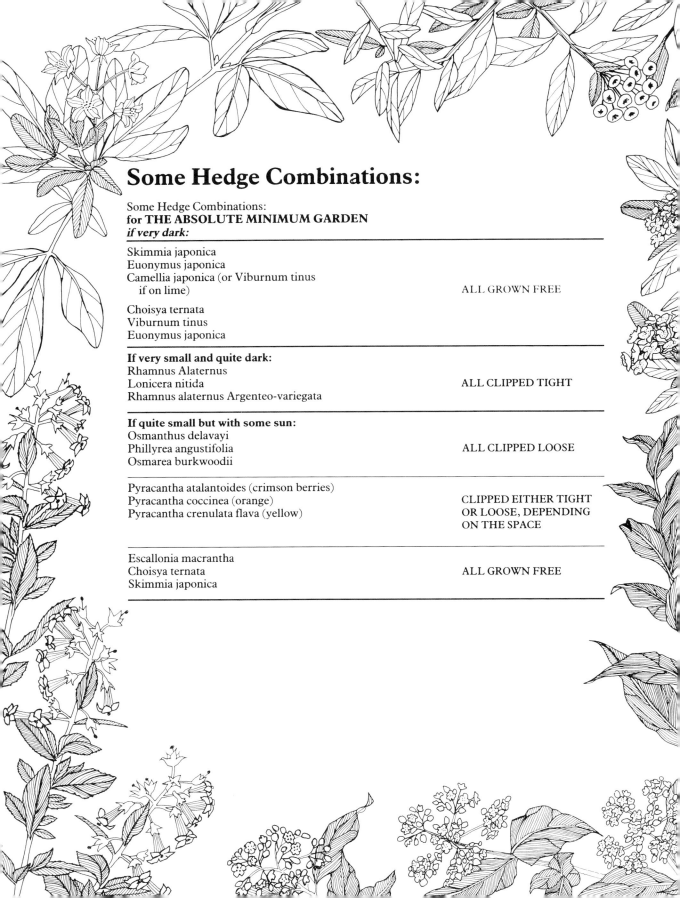

Some Hedge Combinations:

Some Hedge Combinations:
for THE ABSOLUTE MINIMUM GARDEN
if very dark:

Skimmia japonica	
Euonymus japonica	
Camellia japonica (or Viburnum tinus if on lime)	ALL GROWN FREE
Choisya ternata	
Viburnum tinus	
Euonymus japonica	

If very small and quite dark:	
Rhamnus Alaternus	
Lonicera nitida	ALL CLIPPED TIGHT
Rhamnus alaternus Argenteo-variegata	

If quite small but with some sun:	
Osmanthus delavayi	
Phillyrea angustifolia	ALL CLIPPED LOOSE
Osmarea burkwoodii	

Pyracantha atalantoides (crimson berries)	
Pyracantha coccinea (orange)	CLIPPED EITHER TIGHT
Pyracantha crenulata flava (yellow)	OR LOOSE, DEPENDING
	ON THE SPACE

Escallonia macrantha	
Choisya ternata	ALL GROWN FREE
Skimmia japonica	

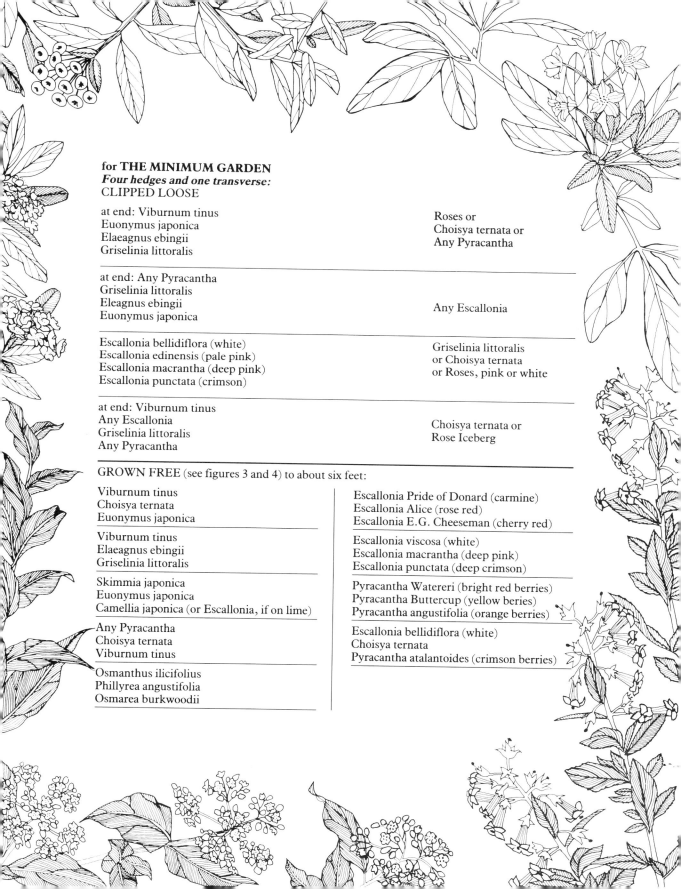

for THE MINIMUM GARDEN
Four hedges and one transverse:
CLIPPED LOOSE

at end: Viburnum tinus
Euonymus japonica
Elaeagnus ebingii
Griselinia littoralis

Roses or
Choisya ternata or
Any Pyracantha

at end: Any Pyracantha
Griselinia littoralis
Eleagnus ebingii
Euonymus japonica

Any Escallonia

Escallonia bellidiflora (white)
Escallonia edinensis (pale pink)
Escallonia macrantha (deep pink)
Escallonia punctata (crimson)

Griselinia littoralis
or Choisya ternata
or Roses, pink or white

at end: Viburnum tinus
Any Escallonia
Griselinia littoralis
Any Pyracantha

Choisya ternata or
Rose Iceberg

GROWN FREE (see figures 3 and 4) to about six feet:

Viburnum tinus
Choisya ternata
Euonymus japonica

Escallonia Pride of Donard (carmine)
Escallonia Alice (rose red)
Escallonia E.G. Cheeseman (cherry red)

Viburnum tinus
Elaeagnus ebingii
Griselinia littoralis

Escallonia viscosa (white)
Escallonia macrantha (deep pink)
Escallonia punctata (deep crimson)

Skimmia japonica
Euonymus japonica
Camellia japonica (or Escallonia, if on lime)

Pyracantha Watereri (bright red berries)
Pyracantha Buttercup (yellow beries)
Pyracantha angustifolia (orange berries)

Any Pyracantha
Choisya ternata
Viburnum tinus

Escallonia bellidiflora (white)
Choisya ternata
Pyracantha atalantoides (crimson berries)

Osmanthus ilicifolius
Phillyrea angustifolia
Osmarea burkwoodii

Opposite
Camellia japonica will grow facing north in acid and neutral soils, but its flowers are destroyed by early morning sun after frost. It should never be clipped.

Rhamnus alaternus and Lonicera nitida make splendid hedges which can be clipped tight. The Rhamnus is of a pleasant middle green, the Lonicera is really dark. Both are hardy and of a fine constitution succeeding almost anywhere, provided the soil is not too poor. The Rhamnus has a variety with a creamy-white variegation on its leaf. It must be firmly clipped from an early age as it can grow enormous.

Four other shrubs with small dark leaves and white, scented flowers would make good hedges tightly clipped. They are Phillyrea angustifolia, from Southern Europe, a very popular hedge, like the Alaternus, in the late seventeenth century; Osmanthus delavayi, which flowers in spring, and Osmanthus ilicifolia, which flowers in autumn, both from China; and Osmarea burkwoodii, a cross between Osmanthus and Phillyrea. They will not flower when clipped tight, but would do so clipped loose. Grown free would need a lot of space and would also, I think, be rather overpowering.

A Minimum Garden. A hedge of the pink-and-white striped Rosa Mundi is planted across the garden to line up with an existing Maple Tree (see figure 6). A hedge of Pyracantha will shortly cover the trunk of the tree. On the left is the dark foliage of the winter-flowering Viburnum tinus, and in the foreground a hedge of Choisya is in flower.

For very small dark gardens, Skimmia japonica is a very helpful shrub. Only to be grown free, as it is rarely more than four feet high (1.20 m.), it has strongly scented flowers in the spring. There are male and female plants, the former with handsomer flowers, the latter with red berries. One male to two females is a good proportion.

If your soil is on the acid side, then Camellia japonica is very accommodating. It should not be clipped, only pruned, and can look very gloomy if allowed to grow too large. It flowers in the very early spring with splendid, scentless flowers, white, pink, scarlet or striped. Very susceptible to morning frosts, it should face south or west if the flowers are to survive the sunrise. It will *grow* facing north, but the flowers will be rarer.

Rose hedges cannot really be recommended for the smaller garden as they look so deeply depressing in the winter. Planted as a transverse hedge, however, against three or four evergreen hedges, they could look extremely beautiful and would re-pay the extra trouble they would cause. They would be at their best in a hedge running north and south – if you stand in your garden towards the end of March or September and find that the sun is setting on your right, then you are facing south. They should all be dead-headed in the summer and either pruned, with secateurs, or clipped with garden shears in early spring. Only one kind of rose should be planted in order to avoid the spotty effect usually achieved by 'Rose Borders' and by no means every kind of rose is suitable for planting as a hedge.

The Hybrid Musks were bred in the first half of this century, having a remote common ancestor in the Himalayan Musk Rose from which they derive their vigour and their scent. Only the smaller ones would be suitable for a Minimum Garden: Buff Beauty, a very subtle shade not quite buff, not quite yellow; Callisto, pale yellow; Cornelia, opening apricot fading to pink; Daybreak, yellow; Felicia, pale pink; Nur Mahal, crimson. They should be pruned with secateurs.

The Gallicas are among the oldest of cultivated roses, notable for their scent and remarkable range of colour, through all shades of pink to crimson and deep purple. Several are handsomely striped. Most of those available to us today were bred in France at the beginning of the last century. They are trouble-free, wonderfully scented and can be clipped with shears in early spring if they get too big.

The Albas are another very ancient group of strongly scented roses, almost completely disease free and needing to be clipped only if they get too big. Felicité Parmentier is pale pink and about four feet high (1.20 m.); Mme. Legras de St. Germain, a superb rich white, can grow to six feet (1.80 m.); the Queen of Denmark is deep pink with especially beautiful grey-green leaves and grows to about five feet (1.50 m.).

The Gallicas and Albas have only one, very generous, flowering season, in the summer. The Hybrid Musks flower then and some of them will continue throughout the summer. For perpetual flowering, the modern rose Iceberg is the best, very white but scentless, keeping its leaves if sheltered from frost and remarkably resistant to disease. As a hedge, it would be better clipped with shears.

All roses like to be well fed in the winter and those mentioned here, with the exception of Iceberg, are better obtained from a rose specialist.

On pages 14 and 15 will be found a number of suggested combinations of the hedging plants mentioned above. As a rough guide, they should all be planted three feet apart (90 cm.), certainly not less than two feet (60 cm.) and four feet (1.20 m.) only when a really vigorous shrub has been chosen.

Figure 5
Plan of a Minimum Garden, with one existing tree. Three hedges of equal length have been planted to make three sides of a square containing it. There should be room for the mower between the hedges and the tree. A hedge of Choisya on the right, with Viburnum tinus across the top. The transverse hedges are of roses – two different Hybrid Musks, for instance, or two different Albas. The hedge between them is of Escallonia.

Trees in the Minimum Garden

You do not plant trees in a Minimum Garden, but there may be
some there already. In general, one tree will be enough and you
must treat it as the focus of your layout plan, placing your hedges
so that the tree looks as if it were meant to be where it is (figure 5).
A tree right at the edge of the garden will grow quite well as part of
the hedge, but the two shrubs on either side of it must be at least
three feet (90 cm.) away from it. Figure 6 shows a way of including
two trees in a Minimum Garden, but you must be sure that they
are not going to grow very large.

If the tree is to grow in grass, make sure that the grass doesn't
strangle it while it is young. Leave a circular bare patch a large
handspan across immediately round its trunk.

Figure 6
Plan of a Minimum Garden,
with two existing trees. A new
hedge, in this case of Choisya,
now leads up to one of them.
(See illustration on page 16).
The other stands in the grass,
but could alternatively be used
as the end of a transverse
hedge. Viburnum tinus on the
left, Escallonia on the right,
Pyracantha across the top, all
clipped loose.

To Plant a Tree or Shrub in Grass

Remove a two-foot square of turf.

Keep enough turf to replace strips six inches wide round the edge of the hole when the tree is planted.

Dig a hole so that the top of it is at the same level as:
(a) the top of your container, or
(b) the point at which the trunk of the tree emerged from the ground before it was dug up.

Put your spare turf face downwards at the bottom of the hole. Chop it up with your spade and add a little bonemeal if you like. Mix them.

Now put in the stake. If you do it after the tree is planted, you may damage its roots.

Then either:
(a) Remove the plastic container very carefully so as not to disturb the soil inside it. Place the plant and the undisturbed soil very gently in the hole and fill in with earth at the sides. Scatter your spare soil very finely over the grass (the rain will wash it in) or elsewhere in the garden. Don't pack it in.
or
(b) Spread the roots towards the sun. Fill in gently with the broken up soil, firming gently as you go, either with your hands or with rubber boots – *no* hobnails. When the hole is full, the level of the soil on the plant should be exactly where it was before, to within half-an-inch.

Leave the surface of the soil loose.

Replace the six inch strips of turf round the edge of the hole.

Tie your plant to the stake, using either a proper plastic tie or thick string having bandaged the plant first. Strips of old jeans are very good for this.

Your plant should now be standing in a square of soil one foot square. Keep weeds and grass away from it.

To Lay Turf

Dig over the area to be turfed to a depth of about six inches.

Rake it well, removing any stones and pebbles and make it as level as possible.

For a Minimum Garden, Meadow Turf will be best.

Lay the turf as you would carpet pieces so that they are touching at the edges but are perfectly flat.

Use a plank to walk over turf you have already laid.

Water it with a hose every day that it doesn't rain, but do not create marsh conditions.

If you have a roller, roll it after about three weeks, before you cut it. If you haven't, ease out any obvious bumps with your plank.

To Sow Grass

Dig over the area to be sown to a depth of about six inches.

Rake it well, removing any stones and pebbles and make it as smooth and level as possible.

Roll the area, if you have a roller. If not, firm it down by laying a plank on the ground and walking on it.

For a Minimum Garden, Second Class Lawn Seed will be best.

Scatter the seed in late March or September, just after a new moon.

Rake it in gently. A wire rake is best.

Water it with a hose every day that it doesn't rain, but don't drown it.

If the area is not too huge, cut it with shears the first time. Otherwise, fix the blades of your mower as high as possible.

BULBS IN THE ONE HOUR GARDEN

One of the features of a One Hour Garden is a well-defined shape of grass longer than the lawn. In this can be grown bulbs, which flower in the spring, and shrubs, which flower in the summer, and which look better confined to a definite shape – say a circle or a square – of longer grass than they do scattered around an immaculate lawn. It is important that the long grass should have an agreeable shape, as it will be unwise to cut it before the early summer, the middle of June in England, by which time the bulbs will have had a chance to die down.

This, in a small garden, will be the one disagreeable chore, as it may well have to be done by hand, either with shears or a sickle. After that it should be possible to maintain the longer grass with the blades of your mower fixed high. There are now many kinds of mower which have several different positions. In a really large garden it may well be worth having a separate machine for the long grass. This should be cut as low as possible when being given its final cut before the winter, so that the small bulbs may have a better chance in the spring.

Pages 26 and 28 are tables of different kinds of bulb that are easy to grow, and the number required to the square foot (30 cm.). Having staked out your area with some string, throw the bulbs concerned *very gently* into that area and plant them exactly where they fall. This will give a natural look when they come up. There are things called 'bulb-planters' – not unlike those things for cutting out pastry cases – which are not expensive and it is probably worth investing in one. Otherwise it must be done with the corner of a spade, or by lifting the turf off the area in question, throwing in the bulbs and then re-laying the turf *very gently* on top of them. Clearly this would only be advisable if the area concerned were quite small.

Digging up bulbs from grass is even more of a labour than planting them, so make quite sure that you are putting what you want where you want it. Once they are there, they are there. Plant the tall ones (which conveniently flower later) towards the centre of your shape, with the smaller, earlier ones nearer the edge.

Bulbs in the One Hour Garden

Opposite: Flowering in very early Spring, late February and early March in England

1. The Winter Aconite (Eranthis hyemalis) is usually the first indication that the winter is over. It is a charming little flower, bright yellow, three to four inches high (7.5 to 10 cm). Plant one inch (2.5 cm.) deep and about two inches (5 cm.) apart, approximately sixteen to a square foot (30 cm. square).

2. The Snowdrop (Galanthus nivalis) is about six inches tall (15 cm.), single or double, white with green markings. There is a giant variety, Galanthus elwesii, which flowers a bit later. They will grow in the grass but do not spread as quickly as they would under trees in a wood, for instance. In a small garden, this is no disadvantage. Plant a little more than an inch deep (3 cm.), about sixteen to the square foot (30 cm. square).

3. Yellow Hoop Petticoat (Narcissus bulbocodium conspicuus) is a bright yellow miniature daffodil about six inches (15 cm.) high. Plant just over one inch (3 cm.) deep, sixteen to the square foot (30 cm. square).

4. February Gold (a Narcissus cyclamineus hybrid). Yellow with a touch of orange in the trumpet. Up to twelve inches (30 cm.) high. Plant two inches (5 cm.) deep, nine to the square foot (30 cm. square).

5. The Lent Lily (Narcissus pseudo-narcissus), the native daffodil. Two shades of pale yellow. About twelve inches (30 cm.) high. Plant two inches (5 cm.) deep, nine to the square foot (30 cm. square).

   There are many other kinds of early dwarf daffodil, all extremely beautiful.

6. Crocuses. The Golden Yellow Mammoth is better planted alone, or mixed only with white and yellow. The usual purple and orange jumble is a bit much in a small garden. The following is a good mixture:

Dark purple (The Bishop)	30%
Dark blue (Remembrance)	30%
Mid blue (Jubilee)	15%
Lilac stripes (Pickwick)	15%
White (Joan of Arc)	10%
or	
Cream (Chrysanthus Cream Beauty)	10%

   These crocuses grow to four or five inches (10 to 12 cm.). Plant two inches (5 cm.) deep, nine to the square foot (30 cm. square).

7. Hybrid Daffodils. There are so many of these that you must make your own choice. They grow to about eighteen inches (45 cm.), sometimes taller. They should be planted about three inches deep (7.5 cm.), four to the square foot (30 cm. square). Two of the earliest are Carlton and Covent Garden.

8. Waterlily Tulips (Tulipa kaufmanniana) grow about eight inches (20 cm.) high and come in wonderful shades of white, cream, yellow and red. Plant two inches (5 cm.) deep, nine to the square foot (30 cm. square).

Bulbs in the One Hour Garden

Opposite: Flowering mid to late spring, April and May in England

1. Hybrid Daffodils. A sequence is suggested below, but there are many other possibilities.

Early April	Cragford and Carbineer
Mid April	Actaea and Geranium
Late April	Golden Perfection and Jonquil Single
Late May	Pheasant's Eye

2. Hybrid Tulips. These are only relatively happy in grass, having a tendency to disappear after their first year. They are well worth trying, however, and can easily be renewed in a small garden every year, twenty or thirty at a time. They come in all colours except blue and brown. If you are keeping to yellow and white, Pax (white) and Golden Melody will flower together early in April, and Asta Nielsen (yellow) and Maureen (white) will do so in late April. Four to the square foot (30 cm. square), about two inches (5 cm.) deep.

3. Tulipa sylvestris, the native tulip, increasingly available from specialist bulb growers. Bright yellow, it is by far the best for growing in grass. About a foot high (30 cm.), nine to the square foot (30 cm. square), about an inch and a half (4 cm.) deep.

4. The Summer Snowflake (Leucojum aestivum). Like an enormous Snowdrop, up to eighteen inches (45 cm.) or more, it flowers late in April or early in May. Plant about three inches (7.5 cm.) deep, three to the square foot (30 cm. square).

5. The Common Bluebell (Scilla campanulata). Blue or white in Nature, there are now some magnificent pink hybrids. Normally ten inches to a foot (25 to 30 cm.) high, they are not always so tall in grass. The new hybrids are much taller. Six to the square foot (30 cm. square), two inches (5 cm.) deep.

6. The Snakeshead Fritillary (Fritillaria meleagris). White, marbled in shades of lilac, and dark purple. About nine inches (22.5 cm.) high, plant two inches (5 cm.) deep, four to the square foot (30 cm. square). But plant a pilot group first as they are particular as to soil, which they prefer to be light.

7. The Crown Imperial (Fritillaria Imperialis). Superb orange, yellow and red, about two feet (60 cm.) in grass. Plant a foot (30 cm.) away from each other, about three inches (7.5 cm.) deep.

The quantities given here are for the small garden where they will be planted only in tens or dozens. For large gardens they can quite safely be halved (except for the Crown Imperial).

THE ONE TREE GARDEN

This should be at least forty-five feet (13.50 m.) long and eighteen (5.40 m.) or twenty feet (6 m.) wide. If you are planting the tree yourself, it should be at the end of the garden furthest from the house. An area of longer grass can be made round it, in which bulbs and, in a slightly larger garden, flowering shrubs can be planted.

The two easiest shapes for this longer grass are a circle or a square. Their centres should be in the centre of your garden. Take a rope and measure the width of your garden. Then put one end in a corner and the rope down the side (as in the Minimum Garden). Diagonals taken from the two corners to the points on the opposite walls will give you, where they cross, the centre of your circle or your square.

In a garden eighteen feet (5.40 m.) wide, two feet (60 cm.) should be allowed for the hedge on each side, and there should be three feet (90 cm.) of mown grass in front of them. Your square of longer grass is thus eight feet square (2.40 m.), or the radius of your circle – preferable in smaller gardens – is four feet (1.20 m.) (fig.7).

This is the minimum size for an area of longer grass. In a smaller garden, the grass will look better at one length, lawn length. In this case the tree may be planted at the centre point discovered above. If it is going into a circle or square of longer grass, it is better not at the centre, but slightly further away from the house, still on the centre line.

In the eight foot square (2.40 m.), or the four foot circle (1.20 m.), only bulbs should be planted, as there is not enough room for the tree *and* shrubs. The minimum size for this is a square of twelve feet (3.60 m.), or a circle of six foot radius (1.80 m.).

Additional Hedges for the One Tree Garden

All the hedges suggested for the Minimum Garden can be used in a One Tree Garden but, as they will not be the only plants, some of the hedges can be deciduous – that is to say, which lose their leaves

Figure 7
Plan of a One Tree Garden. A Medlar tree, planted beyond its centre, stands in a circle of longer grass containing only bulbs. The hedge at the top is partially shaded by the tree, so it should be of a plant that does not need full sun.

in autumn. This can only really be recommended in smaller gardens if (a) the one tree is evergreen or (b) the transverse hedge is evergreen or (c) if the square or circle of longer grass is large enough to contain some evergreen shrubs, that is to say a square of 12 feet (3.60 m.) or a circle with a radius of six feet (1.80 m.).

Assuming that one of the above conditions has been fulfilled, then three native British plants will make a marvellous combination, especially in the autumn.

The Hedge, or Field, Maple (Acer campestre) makes a dense, elegant hedge if clipped tight. It will make a beautiful small tree if grown free. It turns gold in the autumn and would be better used as a background in the smaller garden, that is to say planted across the width of the garden at the top.

The Common Dogwood (Cornus sanguinea) is a much underrated plant from which arrows were made in the Middle Ages. It should be clipped loose, to allow it to flower and then form heads of almost black berries. It turns a soft crimson in the autumn.

The Guelder Rose (Viburnum opulus) – which is not a rose at all – would also be better clipped loose. It has heads of white flowers in late spring or early summer, producing bright red, shiny berries later on. The leaves turn scarlet in the autumn. There is a variety with yellow berries, Viburnum opulus Xanthocarpum.

Fruit Trees for the One Tree Garden

If you are planting only one tree, in a declining economy suddenly very conservation conscious, it should be a fruit tree. Fruit trees should produce fruit which has to be picked, and quite possibly cooked, so The Kitchen must be consulted before any rash steps are taken. Fruit trees also have to be pruned occasionally – so there is *some* maintenance on them – and this is best done (with the exception of plum trees which are better left alone) on a mild day very early in winter. Never do anything in your garden in really cold weather. If it's too cold for you, it's too cold for them.

Lone Fruit Trees, Self-Fertile

Many fruit trees need cross-pollination so can only be planted close to some suitable friends; but some will pollinate themselves and these will be ideal for the One Tree Garden. Half-standard trees are probably the best size for such a garden.

The Common Quince

The Common Quince (Cydonia oblonga *not* the Japanese one, Chaenomeles japonica) is one of the most beautiful small trees that grows in England. Its leaves are a pale green, its flowers pink and the present varieties fruit remarkably early in life. The fruit is like a pear, hard, unyielding and uneatable, but it is absolutely delicious cooked. Picked dry in mid to late autumn, it will keep in a cool place for several months. It can be baked like an apple; it makes superb jelly and jam, chutney, tarts and cheese; it can be grated into apples to be stewed (transforming them utterly) and over pork chops to be grilled. There are four varieties principally available: Champion, Meech's Prolific, Portugal and Vranja, the fruit of the last being perhaps the largest.

The Black Mulberry

The Black Mulberry (Morus nigra) is slow to fruit and probably only worth planting if you mean to remain with it for at least ten years. It is handsome even as a small bush, with large heart-shaped leaves, and its fruit is one of the most delicious of our soft fruits, unpopular with commerce because it travels very badly. It can be eaten raw, or can make jam, jelly or wine and an especially good late Summer Pudding (with Late Summer Raspberries). Unjustly neglected, it is nevertheless not an easy tree to establish. Once it is so, however, it will increase in size and beauty every year, finally getting very large.

The Medlar (Mespilus germanica) makes a very beautiful small tree. If you are short of space this might be the one for you. It has large white flowers as spring turns into summer and its leaves go russet in the autumn. Its fruit makes a delicious jelly. Dutch has the largest leaves, Nottingham the best flavour, but the fruit of Royal is larger. Grand Sultan makes the neatest tree.

There are two self-pollinating Cherries. The first one, Kentish Red, makes a tall tree with leaves which turn scarlet in the autumn. The fruit ripens in early midsummer, bright red, but suitable only for cooking. The second, Morello, makes a smaller tree, rather wider than high, and very dense. The fruit does not ripen until late summer, a very dark red, almost black. It is sharp in flavour and *can* be eaten raw, but is better cooked. The fruit of both these trees make delicious jams, jellies and tarts and, as it also bottles very well, may also be suitable for freezing.

There are several self-fertile members of the Plum family. All will make handsome trees, frequently of an irregular, interesting shape and will not need pruning for many years. When this is required, it is better to be done professionally. The problem with plums is that they bloom very early, so are better planted in a place that is not too windy and is not subject to late frosts.

Victoria is a very reliable lady, not too fussy about position, and producing very regularly a red fruit that can be cooked or eaten.

Marjorie's Seedling ripens very late, in mid-autumn. A large black cooking plum, it makes a particularly good tree, very upright and therefore suitable for the narrow garden.

Czar is another very vigorous cooking plum, purple black, the tree again very upright.

Laxton's Supreme and Oullin's Gage have large, golden-yellow fruit, delicious eaten when ripened by a hot summer, but suitable for cooking even in a normal one.

The Pershore Egg Plum is yellow and only suitable for cooking. As a tree it is remarkably resistant to disease, producing fruit in such quantities as to be almost embarrassing.

The Common Medlar

Opposite
The Mexican Orange, Choisya ternata, will grow almost anywhere provided it is sheltered from the wind. It should be pruned only when it gets too large, never clipped.

Overleaf
The superb apple-green leaves of Griselinia littoralis, better considered as tender in inland districts. It should be pruned when necessary, not clipped.

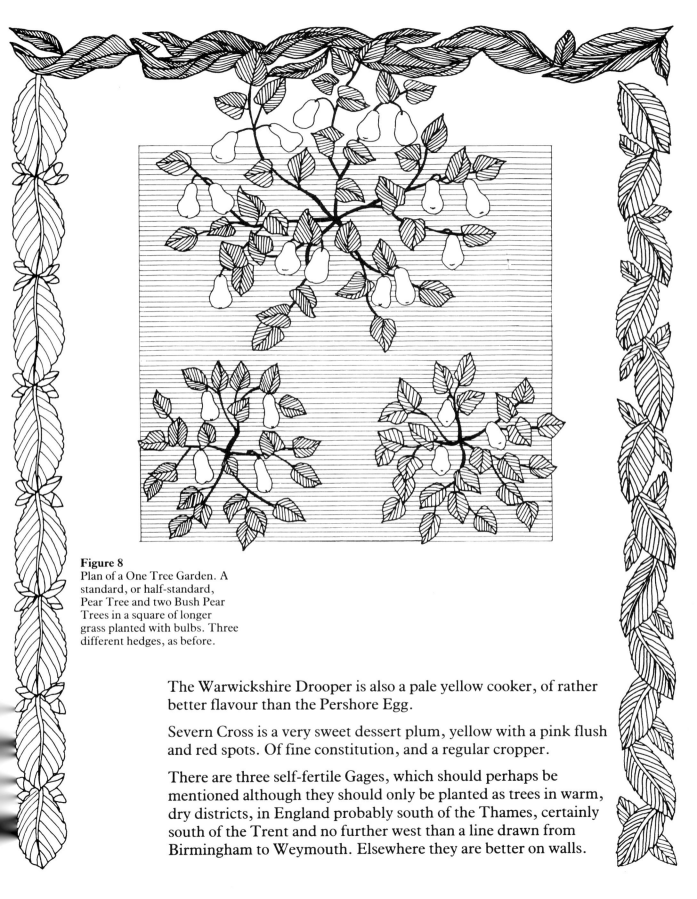

Figure 8
Plan of a One Tree Garden. A
standard, or half-standard,
Pear Tree and two Bush Pear
Trees in a square of longer
grass planted with bulbs. Three
different hedges, as before.

The Warwickshire Drooper is also a pale yellow cooker, of rather
better flavour than the Pershore Egg.

Severn Cross is a very sweet dessert plum, yellow with a pink flush
and red spots. Of fine constitution, and a regular cropper.

There are three self-fertile Gages, which should perhaps be
mentioned although they should only be planted as trees in warm,
dry districts, in England probably south of the Thames, certainly
south of the Trent and no further west than a line drawn from
Birmingham to Weymouth. Elsewhere they are better on walls.

Denniston's Superb is hardy and reliable, making a very upright tree.

Early Transparent Gage is extremely delicious but does need a good summer to ripen properly. It makes a neat, compact tree.

Reine Claude de Bavay ripens late, in early autumn, producing large greenish-yellow fruit on a tree of moderate size.

In some ways the Cherry Plums and Damsons are most suitable for the One Tree Garden, as they are extremely hardy, highly ornamental and very easy to grow. Their fruit is small and, in general, too sour to be eaten but all make excellent jam and are well worth the trouble of picking, which can be considerable.

Merryweather is probably the best damson as it makes a tougher tree than the Shropshire Prune Damson, which has the better flavour.

The Yellow Cherry Plum is very hardy, suitable even for windy sites. It makes a handsome tree, round and with wide branches.

Conference is probably the most reliable of the self-fertile Pears, though its fruit has a better flavour if cross-pollinated. It is the most trouble-free of the Pears, making an upright, very regular tree, highly ornamental both in flower and fruit. It blossoms early so is not really suitable for windy places.

Packham's Triumph is a delicious eating pear, making a small tree very suitable for the small garden.

Fondante d'Automne is a very juicy eating pear, ripening late. It also makes a small tree.

Improved Fertility, despite its rather rude name, is a pear of good flavour, perhaps better cooked than eaten.

There are only two self-fertile Apples. One, the Crawley Beauty, is a particularly delicious cooking apple, blossoming late so suitable for windy sites and frost pockets. The other, Grenadier, is also a cooker with large, greenish yellow fruit. It is an excellent pollinator for other apples.

Figure 9
Plan of a One Tree Garden. Four self-fertile Bush Fruit Trees in a square of longer grass. In a much larger garden half-standards could be used in the same way.

More Ambitious Fruit Trees in the One Tree Garden

If you want to grow fruit trees other than those mentioned above, then you must have room in your garden for a tree and two large bushes in the rough grass (figure 8). The twelve foot (3.60 m.) square is the minimum size for this. If, however, you have as much room as that, then another possibility is for four 'bush fruit trees', one at each corner of the square (figure 9). A bush fruit tree, as they are known in the trade, is a tree with a very short trunk, branching low and ultimately no larger than a bush, say eight feet high (2.40 m.).

The subject of cross-pollination in fruit is rather too large to be attempted here, but in general it can be said that if you have room for only one tree and two bush trees you will be wisest to stick to Apples. They make less complicated trees than plums and fruit more frequently than pears.

A particularly good trio would be, for instance, the Rev. William Wilks, a delicious cooker of unusual fertility as the tree, with Egremont Russet, a hardly reliable eater, and Lord Lambourne, another succulent eater very easy to grow, as the bushes.

Otherwise, any three, or four, of the following will cross-pollinate:

Ashmead's Kernel, an old greenish yellow russet apple which keeps very well.

Blenheim Orange makes a beautiful tree, so should not be grown as a bush. One of the most delicious of the 'old' apples.

Charles Ross is a large, delicious eater, very healthy, not objecting to chalky soils, which some apples do.

Cox's Orange Pippin is really only happy in the south in England and requires more attention than some other apples.

Crispin is very juicy, a very regular and generous cropper, and is probably better grown as a tree.

Discovery, crisp and juicy, would make a good bush.

Epicure is a marvellous apple, very resistant to frost. Perhaps better as a bush as it must be eaten at once.

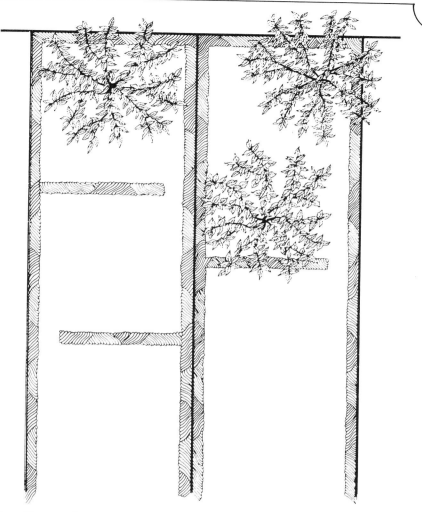

Figure 10
Plan of Two One Hour
Gardens, side by side, both
rather long and thin. The one
on the left has been divided by
transverse hedges into three
squares, with a single tree in
the furthest one. The one on
the right has simply been cut in
half by a transverse hedge, and
two trees planted beyond it.
The trees are three cross-
pollinating Fruit Trees, planted
in neighbourly collaboration.

Golden Russet is not too vigorous, so makes an excellent bush.

Holstein is not unlike a Cox, but is less difficult to grow. It makes a fine tree.

James Grieve and Red James Grieve are large and delicious, particularly good in North Britain as they are resistant to frost. They bruise easily, so do not let them fall.

Merton Russet is a green eating apple which keeps particularly well and fruits generously.

The Sturmer Pippin originated in Essex. It ripens very late and should be left on the tree as long as possible. Very crisp and keeps well.

Sunset makes a neat tree, so is good for the small garden. A seedling from Cox's Orange Pippin, it tastes very much like it but is less trouble to grow. It is especially beautiful in flower.

Tydeman's Early, as one would suppose, is one of the earliest to ripen. It is also very resistant to frost, but has a tendency to fruit only every other year.

Tydeman's Late Orange is quite the opposite, ripening late and cropping regularly and generously. Also a Cox descendant.

Worcester Pearmain is an old, reliable favourite, ripening early.

Wagener is very hardy and free fruiting. It can be eaten or cooked and keeps well.

All the foregoing are Eating Apples. Among the cookers, Bramley's Seedling is probably the best. It makes an enormous, very handsome tree and needs two pollinators, Cox's Orange Pippin and Worcester being the usual choice. More or less any two of the eating apples mentioned above will do, but it is always wise to check with your supplier.

Arthur Turner is a very early, delicious large apple, ripening in mid-summer but staying on the tree until early autumn.

Grenadier is another early, very reliable apple, an excellent pollinator for the Bramley.

Howgate Wonder is very hardy and a reliable, regular cropper with a very good flavour.

N.B. The Blenheim Orange, Bramley's Seedling, Crispin and Holstein are all very poor pollinators and only one of these should be included in any grouping.

Probably the easiest way to grow plums would be to plant any three of the self-fertile varieties previously mentioned. Two of the most delicious dessert plums, Kirke's Blue and Coe's Golden Drop, will pollinate each other and could be grown as bushes in the south of England, though really better on a wall. The other two worth mentioning are Early Laxton, a small golden plum for eating, and River's Early Prolific, a very good cooking plum, both of which ripen early and which also pollinate each other. These should be planted as bushes, with any of the self-fertile varieties as the tree.

Dessert Apple in flower and fruit.

Dessert Plum in flower and fruit.

Dessert Cherry in flower and fruit.

If you are fond of Cherries, grow Morello as the tree and any two of the following as the bushes: Bigarreau Napoleon (pale yellow), Bradbourne Black (dark red), Merton Bigarreau (very dark red), Merton Favourite (dark crimson) and Merton Glory (pale cream). These are all superb eating varieties and, as bushes, are more easily netted against the birds.

If you are serious about Pears, probably the best way is to grow three or four as bushes (figure 9). Standard pears, while making very handsome trees, take a long time to produce any fruit.

With Conference, Fondante d'Automne and Packham's Triumph:

Baronne de Mello, easy to grow, producing a rather small, very juicy fruit.

Josephine de Malines makes a good bush, producing a very sweet fruit which can be ripened indoors.

William's Bon Chretien is also easy to grow, and fruits generously. Liable to scab, it must be sprayed. The fruit is also better picked green and ripened in the house.

With Improved Fertility:
Beurre Hardy, very delicious and vigorous, so it can also be planted as a tree.

Doyenne du Comice, perhaps the most delicious of all, ripening late.

Dessert Pear in flower and fruit.

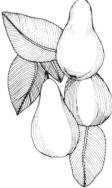

Glou Morceau is green and large, ripening to almost yellow.

Gorham fruits frequently and heavily, the fruit having a very white flesh and an almost russet skin.

Pears are also better protected from the birds. Nets are a nuisance but, on four bush trees, not out of the question.

Finally, there are things called Family Trees. These are trees with three varieties of Apple or Pear grafted on to them, carefully chosen for cross-pollination and balanced growth. In a very small garden, that might be the One Tree to grow.

Small Decorative Trees for the One Tree Garden

If you have room for only one tree in your garden, and cannot be bothered with fruit trees, then, ideally, it should be one that flowers in spring or summer, has berries and coloured leaves in the autumn, and makes an interesting shape, with an interesting bark, so that there is something to look at in the winter. It should also, ultimately, not be too big.

The Whitebeam (Sorbus aria) with several varieties, and the Rowan, or Mountain Ash (Sorbus aucuparia) again with several varieties, are two native trees which more or less fulfil these conditions.

The Whitebeam makes a handsome, solid tree with silver undersides to the leaves. It will tolerate wind and industrial conditions, has bunches of creamy flowers in late spring followed by fruit of a soft scarlet in the autumn.

The Rowan makes a much more open tree, much smaller, with feathery leaves and creamy flowers, followed by red, yellow or orange berries, depending on which variety you choose.

The Whitebeam grows wild on chalk downs, while the Rowan prefers damp moorland, so choose your tree to suit your soil. Both grow well in towns.

The native Hawthorns are very slow growing and look rather ugly in the winter, but their relation Cratageus × lavallei (or carrieri), a hybrid Cockspur Thorn, is a very neat, solid small tree with bunches of white flowers in spring and bright reddish-orange berries. It keeps its quite large leaves well on into the autumn.

The Bird Cherry (Prunus padus) is a very elegant open tree with spikes of white flowers in the spring. There is also a variety with purple flowers (Colorata). The species is a native tree, tolerant of wind and very hardy. The fruit is edible and nearly black, much appreciated by our Stone Age ancestors. Nowadays it is principally popular with the birds.

These are as close as one can come to 'foolproof' trees. If you have room for shrubs, your tree should be planted to the north of them, so that it does not overshadow them. It is especially important in a

Figure 11
Plan of a One Tree Garden. A decorative tree, in this case a Gingko, is accompanied by a pair of shrubs, in this case a kind of Yucca. A transverse hedge, leaving room at the right to pass through, converts the top of the garden into a square with the circle in the middle of it. This is the most elaborate plan for a One Tree Garden, and the suggestions for selecting plants – opposite the plant drawings further on – may be taken as applying to it.

small garden to choose shrubs which harmonise with the tree. There are illustrations in this book which suggest suitable shrub companions for most of the trees mentioned, and a table on pages 65-67 for those that are not illustrated.

In a small garden it may be better to have two of the same shrub (figure 11) and there is a section on shrubs beginning on page 62. The simplest way is probably to choose your tree first and then the shrub that you like best to go with it.

Of the Laburnums, the so-called Scotch Laburnum (Laburnum alpinum) is the easiest to grow and makes the handsomest tree. It has pale yellow, scented, hanging flowers in the very early summer – rather after the other Laburnums – but not too many of them. A relation, Laburnum anagyroides Aureum, has golden leaves, though they sometimes revert to green. It is worth remembering that the seeds of all the Laburnums are poisonous. If you have children, don't have Laburnums.

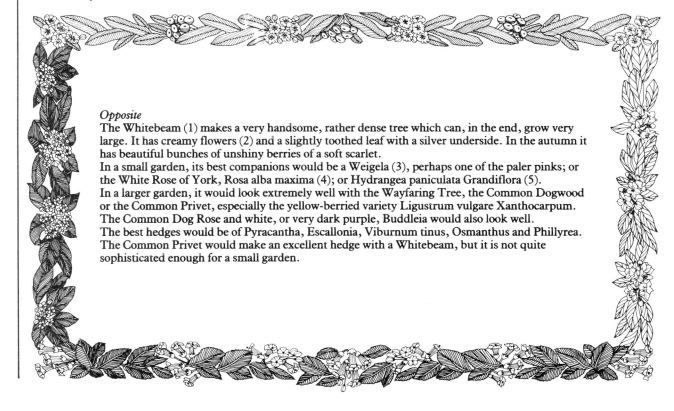

Opposite
The Whitebeam (1) makes a very handsome, rather dense tree which can, in the end, grow very large. It has creamy flowers (2) and a slightly toothed leaf with a silver underside. In the autumn it has beautiful bunches of unshiny berries of a soft scarlet.
In a small garden, its best companions would be a Weigela (3), perhaps one of the paler pinks; or the White Rose of York, Rosa alba maxima (4); or Hydrangea paniculata Grandiflora (5).
In a larger garden, it would look extremely well with the Wayfaring Tree, the Common Dogwood or the Common Privet, especially the yellow-berried variety Ligustrum vulgare Xanthocarpum.
The Common Dog Rose and white, or very dark purple, Buddleia would also look well.
The best hedges would be of Pyracantha, Escallonia, Viburnum tinus, Osmanthus and Phillyrea.
The Common Privet would make an excellent hedge with a Whitebeam, but it is not quite sophisticated enough for a small garden.

The Fig Tree (Ficus carica) is a much hardier tree than people think, though it is unlikely to fruit grown free at the end of your garden. It has enormous leaves the size of one's hand, deeply indented, and makes a tree of very interesting shape up to about fifteen feet (4.50 m.). It likes buildings and is particularly happy in London.

If you are looking for something 'exotic' that is also easy to grow, then the Chinese Angelica Tree (Aralia chinensis or elata) is your plant. Its stems have spines, or large thorns, and therefore should not be grown in conjunction with small children. But its leaves are enormous, deeply cut – 'compound' is the botanical word – up to four feet long and two feet wide (1.20 × .60 m.). It has huge plumes, or sprays – 'panicles' is the botanical word – of tiny white flowers at the end of the summer. There is a particularly handsome variety with a cream variegation. Its drawback, quite a considerable one, is that, if it is happy, it has a tendency to 'sucker', that is to send up new little plants all over the garden from the end of its roots. This, in a One Hour Garden, might be quite interesting but that is the reason why it is shunned by Keen Gardeners.

Not unlike it is Sorbaria arborea, also from China. It grows to about fifteen feet (4.50 m.), again with large compound leaves and creamy plumes in late summer. It is not quite as spectacular as the Aralia but is blander, having no thorns, and better behaved, staying where it is put. Both seem to be perfectly hardy, the former growing well in Northallerton, by no means the warmest place in Britain.

The Manna Ash (Fraxinus ornus) is a very decorative small tree. It too has compound leaves ('Pinnate'), though not so large as the Aralia and Sorbaria, and broad creamy plumes in the very late spring. The fruit, which is relatively rare, is red, but its principal attraction must be its very regular, elegant shape.

The Judas Tree (Cercis siliquastrum) has little purple pea flowers sometimes close to the trunk before the leaves come, producing purple seed pods later. The leaves are a sort of rounded heart-shape and the whole tree has great style, with no drawbacks. There

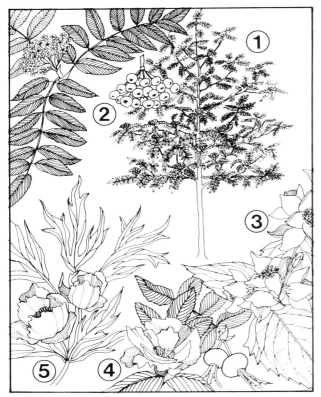

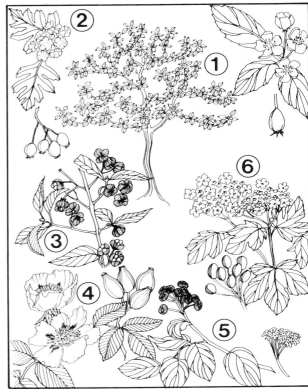

Top left

The Mountain Ash, or Rowan (1), makes a charming, feathery small tree very suitable for the smaller garden. It can be planted quite close to the house as it casts only a light shade. It has creamy flowers (2) and very elegant pinnate leaves. The berries are red, orange or yellow depending on the variety.

All the Philadelphuses (3) look well with the Mountain Ash, especially the golden-leaved one, Philadelphus coronarius Aureus. So does the Japanese Rosa rugosa alba (4) and the yellow-flowered Paeonia lutea ludlowii (5). All the Elders, green and golden-leaved, would look marvellous associated with this tree, as would the Spindleberry, the Guelder Rose and the Dog Rose.

The best hedge would be of Pyracantha in several varieties, or accompanied by Griselinia, Choisya, Elaeagnus ebingii or Euonymus japonica.

Top right

The hybrid Cockspur Thorn, Cratageus × lavallei (1), makes a solid small tree with bunches of white flowers and a slightly shiny leaf, both rather larger than those of the Common Hawthorn (2). This really grows too slowly, and is a little too rustic, for a One Tree Garden. The Cockspur Thorn is best accompanied by unassuming shrubs such as the Spindleberry (3), the Dog Rose (4), the Common Dogwood (5) and the Guelder Rose (6). These would look particularly splendid in the autumn. Weigelas and Hydrangea paniculata Grandiflora would also go well with it.

Pyracantha would be the best hedge for it, either alone – three or four different kinds – or with Griselinia, Escallonia, Choisya, Euonymus japonica and Elaeagnus ebingii.

is a white-flowered variety, with very pale green leaves, now very difficult to find.

Just as distinguished is Idesia polycarpa, a Chinese tree very seldom grown in Britain. It has large heart-shaped leaves with bright red stems and tiny, unnoticeable green flowers. It is sexed, so only the female trees will have bright sprays of red berries in the autumn. It must be thought of here as a 'foliage tree' and a very handsome one. There is a splendid specimen in the Botanical Gardens of Copenhagen, so it must be regarded as hardy throughout Britain, though again not in windy or exposed sites.

The Gingko, or Maidenhair Tree (Gingko biloba), is another very interesting, hardy foliage tree, also from China. It is deciduous, the leaves turning bright yellow in autumn, but has always a most elegant skeleton. Again it is sexed and the One Hour Gardener should grow only the male one. The female has squashy, inedible, evil-smelling fruit which makes a great mess on the ground.

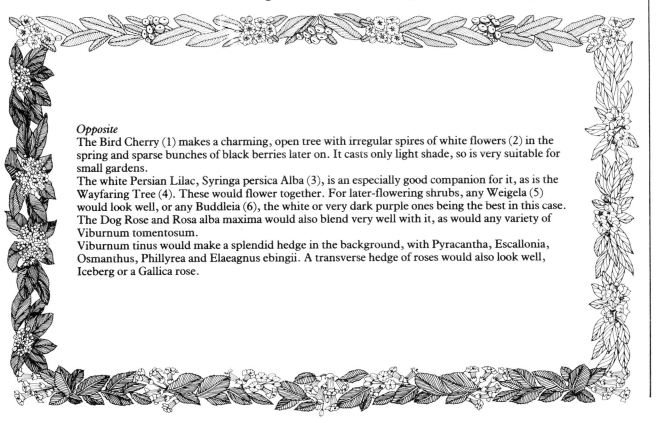

Opposite
The Bird Cherry (1) makes a charming, open tree with irregular spires of white flowers (2) in the spring and sparse bunches of black berries later on. It casts only light shade, so is very suitable for small gardens.
The white Persian Lilac, Syringa persica Alba (3), is an especially good companion for it, as is the Wayfaring Tree (4). These would flower together. For later-flowering shrubs, any Weigela (5) would look well, or any Buddleia (6), the white or very dark purple ones being the best in this case. The Dog Rose and Rosa alba maxima would also blend very well with it, as would any variety of Viburnum tomentosum.
Viburnum tinus would make a splendid hedge in the background, with Pyracantha, Escallonia, Osmanthus, Phillyrea and Elaeagnus ebingii. A transverse hedge of roses would also look well, Iceberg or a Gallica rose.

Finally, if your garden has a rich acid soil, then you can grow the beautiful Eucryphia glutinosa and the Snowdrop Tree (Halesia carolina). Halesia monticola, perhaps even more handsome, will accept a degree of lime. Both have white bell flowers all along their branches in the spring. Carolina is much smaller than monticola, not more than a very large shrub. Monticola in the end makes a tall tree, is particularly hardy and does well in North Britain.

The Eucryphia should only be attempted in a sheltered garden not subject to late frost. It makes a small tree, or large shrub, covered in late summer with white flowers with conspicuous yellow centres and with wonderful autumn colour. It is very upright in shape and also looks well naked.

Flower and leaf of Eucryphia glutinosa

Larger Trees for the One Tree Garden

If your garden is at least twenty feet wide and at least forty feet long – that is to say six metres by twelve – and if your immediate neighbours have no trees in their gardens, then one of the following would be possible. That really is a minimum measurement and, while you could grow shrubs as well while the tree was young, it would eventually swamp them.

Most of these trees come from China or North America, so they are hardy in all but the windiest and coldest sites. If you have one of these, you will be wiser to plant a native tree.

An exception to this is the Box Elder (Acer negundo) also called the Ashleaf Maple. It is a reliable tree in that it is very hardy and not particular about soil, but really only worth planting if you have a 'difficult' garden. It has a variety with golden leaves, Auratum, and one with a cream variegation, Variegatum, and one with a

yellow variegation, Elegantissimum. These are really handsomer than the species but are all liable to revert, that is to say to produce plain green branches among the gold and silver; and the only way to deal with that is to cut back the offending green branch right to the trunk.

The Dove Tree, or the Ghost Tree, or the Handkerchief Tree (Davidia involucrata), is a very graceful tree, tall rather than broad, so well suited to a narrow garden. In the late spring the small flower head emerges purple between pale yellow 'wings', called bracts, which gradually turn white as the flower opens yellow. In flower it is truly spectacular but the leaves are large and heart-shaped and it is at all times a handsome object.

The Magnolias are nearly all extremely beautiful but they are particular about soil, which must be acid and deep, at least three feet (90 cm.). Magnolia kobus, a small Japanese tree with creamy-white flowers, and Magnolia sinensis, rather larger and with particularly handsome leaves, will grow on alkaline soils – that is to say on chalk or limestone, but again the soil must be deep and rich.

For acid soils, the hardiest is probably Magnolia tripetala, a North American tree growing up to thirty feet (9 m.), with enormous leaves and curious triangular white flowers, which are followed by red fruit, not unlike fir cones. Magnolia obovata, or hypoleuca, also has large leaves and very large scented flowers, with a ring of crimson stamens in the centre. Native to Japan, it is also very hardy. Magnolia sargentiana has huge pink flowers and large leaves, grey underneath, while Magnolia mollicomata has pinkish purple flowers which it produces relatively young.

All the Magnolias will take some years to flower but they are well worth waiting for; and perhaps this is a good place to mention that all trees with large leaves particularly dislike wind and they should not be planted in gardens with that problem.

Magnolia grandiflora is evergreen with enormous shiny leaves and very large, scented creamy-white flowers in the summer. It is more usually grown against south and west facing walls but will make an extremely dense, handsome free-standing tree in a sheltered urban, or suburban, area. It will grow on lime soils but again must

Opposite
The magnificent leaves of Cornus alba Spaethii, one of the handsomest of the golden-variegated Dogwoods.

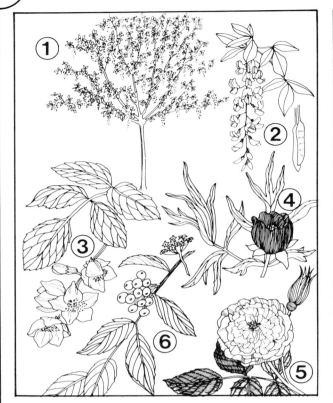

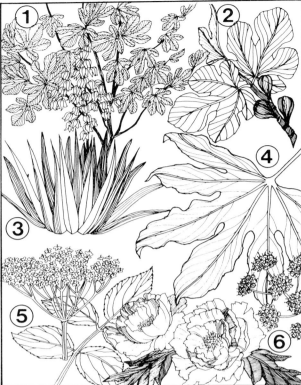

Top left

The Scotch Laburnum, Laburnum alpinum (1), is really the best Laburnum for a One Tree Garden. Its flowers are of a clear yellow and its seeds (2) are poisonous, so do not plant it if you have children. The golden-leaved Philadelphus coronarius Aureus (3) is perhaps its best companion, but the crimson Paeonia delavayi (4) or the yellow Paeonia lutea ludlowii would look extremely well. The yellow Hybrid Musk Rose Buff Beauty (5), with very handsome dark green leaves, or any of the variegated varieties of Cornus alba (6), Cornus mas or Cornus alternifolia Argentea, would also set it off very well. The yellow-flowered Diervillas, sessilifolia and splendens, flowering much later, would harmonise well.

Bright green hedges would probably be best – Pyracantha, Griselinia, Euonymus japonica, Choisya, with Elaeagnus ebingii in the background.

Top right

The Fig (1) makes a very dramatic small tree, interesting to look at at all times, even in the winter. It has very large palmate leaves (2), but is not really likely to fruit in England when grown free. Yucca (3) or Fatsia japonica (4) would certainly be its best, and equally dramatic, companions, but the Fatsia – if there were to be two of them – would take up a lot of room. So would Sambucus canadensis maxima (5), which would look magnificent in front of it. The smaller Elders would also look very well, a hybrid Tree Peony (6), any Hybrid Musk Rose or the Guelder Rose.

A mixture of Pyracanthas and Escallonias would be best as hedges, though Griselinia, Choisya and Euonymus japonica would also look well.

have a good depth. It should also be watered in anything that can possibly be thought of as 'a dry summer'.

The Catalpas, from North America, are so extremely beautiful that one wonders why they are not more generally planted. Catalpa bignonoides, the Indian Bean Tree, has large heart-shaped leaves with large spires of quite large white flowers in the mid to late summer. Catalpa speciosa has equally large leaves and even larger flowers, white with purple spots, though not quite so many of them. There is a golden-leaved variety of Catalpa bignonoides – Aurea – which only rarely makes a tree. Grown as a large bush in a small garden it could be very handsome.

Their Chinese cousin, Catalpa fargesii, is a smaller tree, with smaller flowers, but just as handsome and, for our purposes, perhaps even more suitable. Its flowers are lilac-pink with reddish spots, stained yellow at the throat, also borne in mid-summer.

Catalpas are better planted young and it is most important to keep the grass well away from the trunk. A circle of bare earth about eighteen inches across (45 cm.) should be maintained round each tree.

One of the fastest growing, as well as one of the most beautiful, trees which grows in England is Paulownia fargesii. It has a lilac-coloured flower like a foxglove before the leaves come, in mid to late spring. The leaves are enormous, of a shape difficult to describe (page 81). Its cousin, Paulownia tomentosa, has slightly darker flowers, its leaves are not quite so big and it doesn't grow quite so fast. Either is most acceptable in a One Tree Garden. They have one foolish habit, that of forming their flower buds in the autumn, so that they have the winter to survive before opening in the spring. This, inevitably, sometimes does not happen; but they are well worth growing for their leaves and the shape of the tree.

The Yellow Wood (Cladrastis lutea) is a very elegant, light and graceful tree very infrequently planted. Its one drawback is that the branches are brittle and it is therefore not for windy sites. It has white flowers in early summer, hanging down, and it goes a superb yellow in the autumn. In the winter one can see why it is called Yellow Wood. Its Chinese cousin, Cladrastis sinensis, has a pink tinge to its white flowers.

Another elegant, fast-growing North American tree is the False Acacia (Robinia pseudo-acacia). An excellent tree for people in a hurry, it too has white drooping flowers in the early summer and delicate pinnate leaves. It does, however, drop sharp twigs all over the ground below and to collect these you will require a rake.

A rake is a kind of open-toothed comb on the end of a long handle, and can be obtained in wood, metal or rubber. If your tree is deciduous, you will need one anyway.

Robinia Frisia, a so-called 'sport' of the False Acacia because it appeared by accident, has brilliant yellow foliage, is rather less messy than its parent and would be a wonderful starting point for a Garden of Golden Leaves (table on page 129).

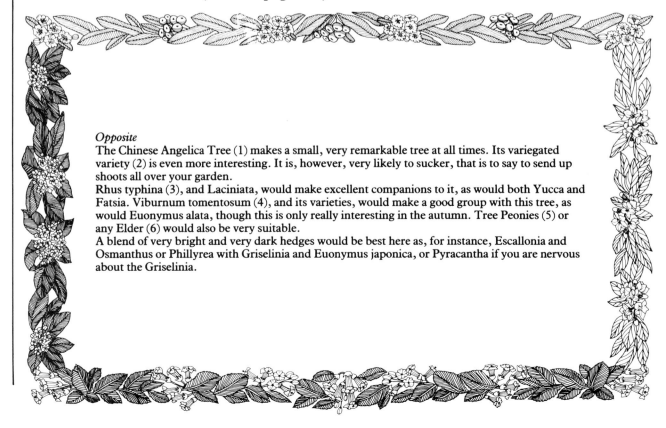

Opposite
The Chinese Angelica Tree (1) makes a small, very remarkable tree at all times. Its variegated variety (2) is even more interesting. It is, however, very likely to sucker, that is to say to send up shoots all over your garden.
Rhus typhina (3), and Laciniata, would make excellent companions to it, as would both Yucca and Fatsia. Viburnum tomentosum (4), and its varieties, would make a good group with this tree, as would Euonymus alata, though this is only really interesting in the autumn. Tree Peonies (5) or any Elder (6) would also be very suitable.
A blend of very bright and very dark hedges would be best here as, for instance, Escallonia and Osmanthus or Phillyrea with Griselinia and Euonymus japonica, or Pyracantha if you are nervous about the Griselinia.

Gleditschia triacanthos Sunburst is another elegant, tough, golden-leaved tree. The species, Gleditschia triacanthos, is extremely hardy and will tolerate even a smoke-polluted atmosphere. It is an elegant tree but with long, strong thorns, and therefore not suitable where there are children. The variety Inermis is thornless.

Two Chinese trees that are very rarely grown in England – perhaps because no one has ever heard of them – are the Amur Cork Tree, (Phellodendron amurense) and Evodia hupehensis (now known as Euodia, a difficult name to pronounce). Both have handsome pinnate leaves and creamy bunches of flowers not too unlike the Whitebeam and the Mountain Ash. But while the Phellodendron produces its flowers in the summer, the Euodia does so in the early autumn, in England in September, practically the only temperate tree to do so. Both will make a broadly-spreading tree of, at the very most, 30 feet or 9 metres wide, but the Euodia is much more solid than the Phellodendron, which is described in at least one reference book as 'gaunt'. It is an open tree, rather graceful, with excellent autumn colour. Both will tolerate chalky soils and may be regarded as hardy if they are not exposed to icy winds. That is to say, they are better in sheltered suburban gardens in the south and west of Great Britain. Both have a handsome bark.

Finally, The Golden Rain Tree, or Pride of India (Koelreuteria paniculata) – which is in fact a native of China – has splendid upright panicles (like a Horse Chestnut) of brilliant yellow flowers in the summer. It has elegantly cut, long pinnate leaves, which unfold red in the late spring and turn yellow before becoming green. In the autumn they turn yellow and brown. It is particularly fond of sun but is not fussy about soil, except that there must be a reasonable depth. The bark is interesting and it is a pleasure to look at, even in the winter.

Not all these trees are very easy to find. At your local garden centre you must be prepared for the 'never 'eard of it'. Even reputable nurserymen will explain that they do not stock it 'because there is no demand for it' and will then suggest another tree which is probably not like it at all. In fact, substitutes will not do in the One Hour Garden. It must be planted with things that other people do not grow and these may well be difficult to find. But it is worth the

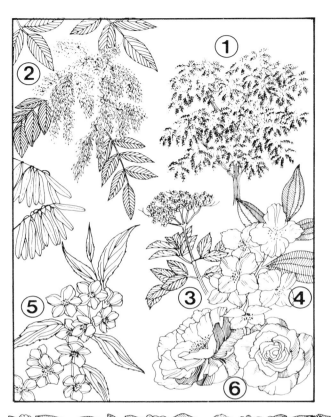

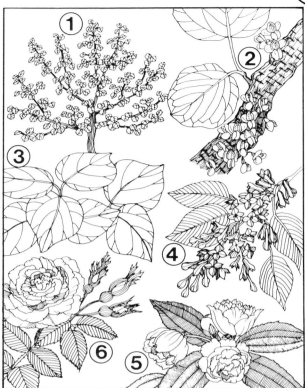

Top left

The Manna Ash (1) makes a very decorative, quite small tree, better to be planted at the far end of a not very large garden. It has amazing plumy white flowers (2) in the spring, followed rather rarely by red fruits. Any of the Elders (3) would look well with it, depending on the space available. Any of the smaller Philadelphuses (4) would blend well, as would the very handsome Deutzia × rosea (5) and its white variety Grandiflora, the rose Iceberg or the Hybrid Musk Prosperity (6). The Weigelas, the Diervillas, the Persian Lilac and the Guelder Rose would all go well with it.

Pyracantha will be the best background hedge, either alone or sharply contrasted with Escallonia and Osmanthus. Choisya or Iceberg, if you have not already used it, would make a charming transverse hedge.

Top right

The Judas Tree (1) makes a very distinguished small tree, rather slow-growing, with pinkish-mauve pea flowers (2) in the spring, sometimes quite close to the trunk, followed by purplish seed pods. If you are on acid soil, Disanthus cercidifolius (3) would be a handsome companion for it, particularly in the autumn. If not, the Persian Lilac (4), or Syringa microphylla, or any of the double Philadelphuses (5), or Rosa alba maxima (6) would look very well with it. Weigela florida in any variety, Deutzia × rosea and pink or white Hybrid Musk Roses would all blend well.

Small-leaved, dark hedges will be best, four kinds of Escallonia, for instance, or Osmanthus and Phillyrea as well, with perhaps Viburnum tinus in the background.

trouble in the end. Even in these days, with the customer always wrong, it is possible to create a demand; and it is, in any case, more than time that there was a revolution in taste in the English Garden.

Shrubs for the One Tree Garden

Let us suppose that you have room in your circle or your square for two or three shrubs. If there are to be two then they should be a pair, if three a pair and a single, otherwise they will look too busy. Calm is one of the great essences of the One Hour Garden.

The Elders are among the most easily grown shrubs, all very good-looking. The Common Elder (Sambucus nigra) is an elegant shrub with creamy-white heads of flower followed by dark purple berries. It should be judiciously pruned, with secateurs, from time to time, otherwise it will grow into a small tree. It will grow in the poorest soil and with relatively little light.

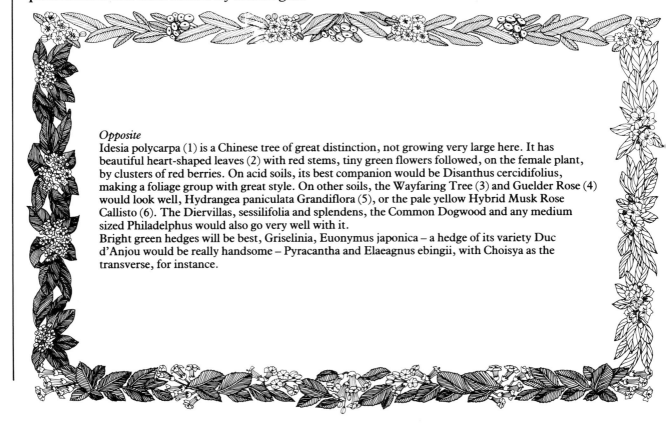

Opposite
Idesia polycarpa (1) is a Chinese tree of great distinction, not growing very large here. It has beautiful heart-shaped leaves (2) with red stems, tiny green flowers followed, on the female plant, by clusters of red berries. On acid soils, its best companion would be Disanthus cercidifolius, making a foliage group with great style. On other soils, the Wayfaring Tree (3) and Guelder Rose (4) would look well, Hydrangea paniculata Grandiflora (5), or the pale yellow Hybrid Musk Rose Callisto (6). The Diervillas, sessilifolia and splendens, the Common Dogwood and any medium sized Philadelphus would also go very well with it.
Bright green hedges will be best, Griselinia, Euonymus japonica – a hedge of its variety Duc d'Anjou would be really handsome – Pyracantha and Elaeagnus ebingii, with Choisya as the transverse, for instance.

Its golden-leaved variety, Sambucus nigra Aurea, is worth a place in any One Hour Garden, as are the two variegated forms, one with white margins, one with yellow. These are all a little less vigorous than the species.

The American Elder (Sambucus canadensis) is larger in every way than the Common Elder, that is to say its flower heads are larger and its leaves are longer. It has a golden leaved variety and a giant relation called Sambucus canadensis maxima, which can grow up to ten feet (3 m.) and which, in the One Tree Garden, would be better regarded as a tree.

The Red Elder (Sambucus racemosa) has scarlet berries, and its variety Plumosa Aurea has deeply cut, golden yellow leaves, rather less vigorous than the species, which will grow to about eight feet (2.40 m.).

The Californian Elder (Sambucus callicarpa) is perhaps the most elegant of the Elders, and it has either scarlet or yellow berries.

Some people find that Elder blossom gives them hay fever but otherwise, given sufficient room to develop, their sole drawback is their fecundity. In a One Hour Garden, however, with no bare earth, the mower will take care of any seedlings.

The two native Viburnums, the Wayfaring Tree (Viburnum lantana) and the Guelder Rose (Viburnum opulus) already mentioned as a hedging plant, are as handsome as the Elders and as easy. The first has very dense cream-coloured heads of flower in early summer, followed by red berries which turn black; and the second has more delicate white flowers, also in early summer, followed by berries as bright and shiny as red currants. There is a variety Xanthocarpum with yellow berries. The Wayfaring Tree has large, rough leaves, the Guelder Rose smaller, smoother ones, which turn red in the autumn. Both these plants can make small trees up to ten feet (3 m.), but respond well to gentle pruning if they seem to be getting too large.

Other Tree and Shrub Combinations for the One Tree Garden (not illustrated)

One Tree and two of any one shrub

Standard Apple, Pear or Cherry	Pink Hybrid Musk Roses Common Dog Rose Smaller Philadelphus Syringa persica Alba Weigela florida, in variety Guelder Rose
Standard Plum or Damson	Common Dog Rose Guelder Rose Common Elder Red Elder Californian Elder Syringa microphylla Double-flowered Philadelphus
Standard Quince or Medlar	Guelder Rose Common Dogwood Wayfaring Tree Common Dog Rose Syringa persica Hydrangea paniculata Grandiflora Paeonia suffruticosa Hybrids
Sorbaria arborea	Buddleia davidii in variety, esp. Black Night Golden Elder Common Elder Red Elder Californian Elder Hydrangea paniculata Grandiflora Paeonia lutea ludlowii and delavayi Diervilla sessilifolia Diervilla x splendens Viburnum tomentosum Any Yucca
Eucryphia glutinosa	Any Hybrid Musk Rose Rose Iceberg Hibiscus syriacus, white flowers only Smaller Philadelphus, single and double Ligustrum delavayanum (evergreen) Syringa microphylla Cotinus coggygria Foliis Purpureis Diervilla sessilifolia Diervilla x splendens Any Yucca

Robinia Frisia and Gleditschia triacanthos Sunburst both with yellow leaves	Sambucus nigra Aurea Sambucus canadensis Aurea Sambucus racemosa Plumosa Aurea Philadelphus coronarius Aureus Yellow Hybrid Musk Roses Paeonia lutea ludlowii Cornus alba Gouchaltii or Spaethii (both with yellow variegation) Viburnum opulus Xanthocarpum (yellow berried Guelder Rose) Ligustrum vulgare Xanthocarpum (yellow berried Common Privet) Diervilla sessilifolia Diervilla x splendens Any Yucca
Sambucus canadensis maxima A giant American Elder	Cornus alba Variegata (silver) Cornus alternifolia Argentea (silver) Cornus alba Gouchaltii or Spaethii (yellow variegation) Hydrangea paniculata Grandiflora Paeonia lutea ludlowii Deutzia x rosea Grandiflora Hybrid Musk Roses Rose Iceberg Syringa persica Alba Buddleia davidii White Bouquet or White Cloud Buddleia fallowiana Alba
Cornus alternifolia Argentea A silver-variegated Dogwood	Common Dog Rose Hybrid Musk Roses Rose Iceberg Rosa alba maxima Buddleia fallowiana Alba Buddleia davidii White Bouquet or White Cloud Smaller Philadelphus, single or double Hydrangea paniculata Grandiflora Weigela florida, in variety Hibiscus syriacus, pink, white or red
Cornus mas The Cornelian Cherry	Common Dog Rose Hybrid Musk Roses Guelder Rose Hydrangea paniculata Grandiflora Syringa persica Alba Cornus alba Gouchaltii or Spaethii Paeonia suffruticosa Hybrids Diervilla sessilifolia Diervilla x splendens

Rhus typhina Rhus typhina Laciniata	Golden Elder Sambucus canadensis Aurea Sambucus racemosa Plumosa Aurea Any green-leaved Elder Smaller Philadelphus, single or double Syringa persica and Alba Rosa rugosa alba Weigela florida, in variety Deutzia x rosea Paeonia lutea ludlowii and delavayi Paeonia suffruticosa Hybrids Any Yucca
Amur Cork Tree Phellodendron amurense Euodia hupehensis	Common Elder Californian Elder Red Elder American Elder Sambucus canadensis maxima Weigela florida in variety, esp. Mont Blanc Diervilla sessilifolia Diervilla x splendens Deutzia x rosea Grandiflora Viburnum tomentosum Paeonia lutea ludlowii and delavayi Paeonia suffruticosa Hybrids Hibiscus syriacus, pink, white and red Hybrid Musk Roses Rose Iceberg Any Yucca
Black Mulberry Morus nigra	Disanthus cercidifolius (acid soils only) Syringa persica and Alba Guelder Rose Common Dogwood Yellow Hybrid Musk Roses Diervilla sessilifolia and splendens Rose Iceberg Weigela florida, all varieties Deutzia x rosea and Grandiflora Any Yucca
Gleditschia triancanthos Inermis Thornless Locust	Syringa persica Alba Buddleia davidii White Cloud or White Bouquet Buddleia fallowiana Alba Smaller Philadelphus Deutzia x rosea and Grandiflora Viburnum tomentosum Dog Rose Rose alba maxima Any Yucca

The evergreen Viburnum tinus, mentioned as a hedge plant for the Minimum Garden, also makes an excellent, free-standing shrub. Its leaves are dark and it has the great advantage of frequently flowering at Christmas. If something a little more sophisticated is wanted, then Viburnum tomentosum, and its varieties, have horizontal branches and red leaves in the autumn; but not all of them have berries. Those of Viburnum tinus are a very dark purplish blue. Nearly all the Viburnums are suitable for a small garden. These are the easy ones.

Of the roses, clearly the easiest of all is the native Dog Rose (Rosa canina) whose variety Andersonii can be found in specialist lists. Lightly pruned, it makes a graceful bush, flowers for as long as any other shrub rose and produces spectacular vermilion hips, from which a nourishing, rather indelicious, syrup can be made.

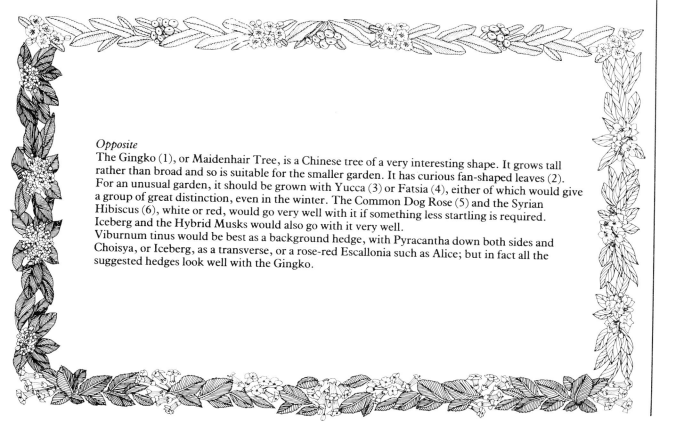

Opposite
The Gingko (1), or Maidenhair Tree, is a Chinese tree of a very interesting shape. It grows tall rather than broad and so is suitable for the smaller garden. It has curious fan-shaped leaves (2). For an unusual garden, it should be grown with Yucca (3) or Fatsia (4), either of which would give a group of great distinction, even in the winter. The Common Dog Rose (5) and the Syrian Hibiscus (6), white or red, would go very well with it if something less startling is required. Iceberg and the Hybrid Musks would also go with it very well.
Viburnum tinus would be best as a background hedge, with Pyracantha down both sides and Choisya, or Iceberg, as a transverse, or a rose-red Escallonia such as Alice; but in fact all the suggested hedges look well with the Gingko.

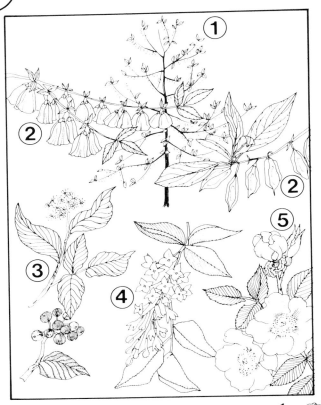

Top left

There are two Snowdrop Trees (1), Halesia monticola – which makes a large tree on almost any soil – and Halesia carolina – which makes a small tree on acid soils only. Both have flowers all along their branches underneath (2) in the late spring, sometimes followed by curious little fruits. Both make rather open trees.

They look well with rather simple, open shrubs, the Common Dogwood (3), the Persian Lilac (4), both mauve and white, and the Common Dog Rose (5). Cornus mas – if you have room as it is really a small tree – looks very well with them, as do all the Philadelphuses except coronarius Aureus, and Viburnum tomentosum and its varieties. A very charming arrangement, needing a lot of space by our standards, would be a grouping of Halesia carolina with Exochorda serratifolia, a very free-flowering shrub with large white flowers. As this will grow on lime, if you have no room for monticola, you could plant it instead of carolina. It grows to about fifteen feet (4.50 m.) and can be associated as above.

Small-leaved, dark hedges will be best, Escallonia, Osmanthus, Phillyrea.

Top right

The Box Elder, or Ashleaf Maple (1) makes a large open tree, recommended only in 'difficult' gardens. It has a particularly beautiful leaf (2), though in some ways the golden-leaved varieties, Acer negundo Auratum and Elegantissimum, and the silver-variegated Acer negundo Variegatum, are more interesting.

They all look better with simple shrubs, the Elders (3) and the Guelder Rose (4) and the Hybrid Musk Roses (5), all of which are easy to grow. Hydrangea paniculata Grandiflora looks well with them all. With the golden-leaved tree, the golden-leaved Elders or Philadelphus coronarius Aureus; Cornus alba Gouchaltii and Spaethii, Cornus mas Elegantissima; and the Hybrid Musk Rose Buff Beauty. With the silver-variegated one, any of the green Elders, Rhus typhina Laciniata, a double-flowered Philadelphus or a white Syrian Hibiscus.

Bearing in mind that this is a 'difficult' garden, I should be inclined to plant only Pyracantha – four different kinds perhaps – as hedges.

The Japanese Rosa rugosa alba is a vigorous shrub, not subject to too many diseases. It is very prickly, has large single white flowers followed by huge red hips like small tomatoes, and its leaves turn yellow in the autumn.

Of the others, the Hybrid Musks, the Gallicas and Albas mentioned previously as Hedging Plants for the Minimum Garden, also make excellent individual shrubs. A favourite of my own is the White Rose of York (Rosa alba maxima), also the Jacobite Rose, which will tolerate a degree of shade.

All the mediaeval and seventeenth century roses, the Gallicas, Albas, Centifolias and Damasks, make well shaped bushes when grown alone in the grass. They are well worth further enquiry as many of them are still available. They flower for about five weeks in the summer, unbelievably generously, but do not all have hips. On the other hand, they do not seem to be subject to blackspot.

The Common Dogwood (Cornus sanguinea), also already mentioned as a hedge plant, makes an elegant bush up to about eight feet (2.40 m.), turning purple, or at least a very dark crimson, in the autumn and having black berries. Variegated shrubs – that is to say shrubs whose green leaves are patterned with cream or yellow, white or pink, usually round the edges – can look well in a small garden provided there are not too many; and foremost among these must be the foreign relations of our native Dogwood.

Cornus alba comes from the Far East and has many interesting varieties. It must be regarded here as a 'foliage shrub' as its principal interest lies in its leaves; and it will also take over your One Tree Garden if you let it. Cornus mas, from Europe, has tiny yellow flowers at the end of the winter, followed by small red fruits much eaten by our Elizabethan ancestors, who called it the Cornelian Cherry. It will make a small tree, up to about ten feet (3 m.), and also has several variegated varieties.

Cornus alternifolia Argentea is one of the handsomest shrubs with a silver variegation. It comes from North America. All the foreign Cornus are vigorous and easy to grow, so much so that they are probably better thought of as trees in the One Tree Garden.

Previous page
The delicately cut leaves of Sambucus racemosa Plumosa Aurea, a Red Elder of great decorative value. Not for people in a hurry.

Opposite
Argenteo-variegata, an extremely beautiful form of Euonymus japonica, which makes a particularly handsome hedge in contrast with very dark greens.

The Common Privet is certainly a foolproof plant, semi-evergreen with black berries. Its flowers have a smell that some people dislike. Probably the best one for a small garden is the kind with yellow berries, Ligustrum vulgare Xanthocarpum. Both these plants make excellent hedges, not quite sophisticated enough to accord with the evergreen hedges suggested for the Minimum Garden. But in a large garden, or a country garden, or a long side of your garden which faces north, the Privet will do you proud.

It has some rather desirable Chinese and Japanese relations, also evergreen. The Chinese one, Ligustrum lucidum, makes a very pretty small tree if you let it. It has a variety with larger leaves – Latifolium – and there are two variegated kinds, Excelsum Superbum, which is marked with dark yellow and white, and Tricolor, marked with white and with pink when young.

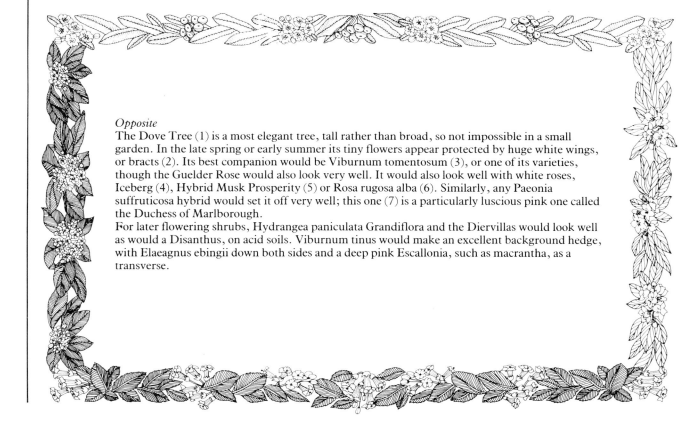

Opposite
The Dove Tree (1) is a most elegant tree, tall rather than broad, so not impossible in a small garden. In the late spring or early summer its tiny flowers appear protected by huge white wings, or bracts (2). Its best companion would be Viburnum tomentosum (3), or one of its varieties, though the Guelder Rose would also look very well. It would also look well with white roses, Iceberg (4), Hybrid Musk Prosperity (5) or Rosa rugosa alba (6). Similarly, any Paeonia suffruticosa hybrid would set it off very well; this one (7) is a particularly luscious pink one called the Duchess of Marlborough.
For later flowering shrubs, Hydrangea paniculata Grandiflora and the Diervillas would look well as would a Disanthus, on acid soils. Viburnum tinus would make an excellent background hedge, with Elaeagnus ebingii down both sides and a deep pink Escallonia, such as macrantha, as a transverse.

Also from China, and especially suitable for the small garden, is Ligustrum delavayanum, a broadly spreading shrub rarely more than six feet (1.80 m.) in height. It will grow in the shade and looks especially handsome when it produces its dense panicles of flowers, white with violet centres.

The Japanese Privet (Ligustrum japonicum), is smaller than lucidum and not quite so vigorous, making a shrub up to about eight feet (2.40 m.). Its two varieties, Macrophyllum and Rotundifolium, have larger leaves, and all three are easy to grow even in the poorest soil, though not, once again, if exposed to a lot of wind.

I cannot really recommend the most usually seen Japanese Privet (Ligustrum ovalifolium) to the One Hour Gardener. Its golden-leaved variety can make a handsome shrub, but as a hedge it can need clipping as many as four times in a damp summer.

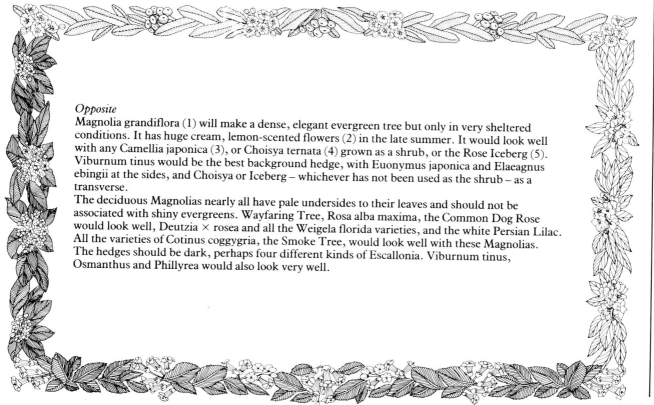

Opposite

Magnolia grandiflora (1) will make a dense, elegant evergreen tree but only in very sheltered conditions. It has huge cream, lemon-scented flowers (2) in the late summer. It would look well with any Camellia japonica (3), or Choisya ternata (4) grown as a shrub, or the Rose Iceberg (5). Viburnum tinus would be the best background hedge, with Euonymus japonica and Elaeagnus ebingii at the sides, and Choisya or Iceberg – whichever has not been used as the shrub – as a transverse.

The deciduous Magnolias nearly all have pale undersides to their leaves and should not be associated with shiny evergreens. Wayfaring Tree, Rosa alba maxima, the Common Dog Rose would look well, Deutzia × rosea and all the Weigela florida varieties, and the white Persian Lilac. All the varieties of Cotinus coggygria, the Smoke Tree, would look well with these Magnolias. The hedges should be dark, perhaps four different kinds of Escallonia. Viburnum tinus, Osmanthus and Phillyrea would also look very well.

All the plants mentioned as making hedges suitable for the Minimum Garden will make elegant bushes for the One Tree Garden. Among the others, the Spindle Tree (Euonymus europaea) is very easy, though unexciting until the autumn. Its relation, Euonymus alata, has a more interesting shape and more spectacular autumn colour, but no berries.

The shrubs so far mentioned all have some kind of winter interest, either evergreen leaves, or berries, or a reasonable shape when bare. We come now to a section of plants grown frankly for their flowers and which do look rather miserable in the winter. In a One Tree Garden, the ideal way would be to screen them with an evergreen transverse hedge (figure 11).

First among these must be the Buddleias (the Butterfly Bushes), not all of which are perfectly hardy. Buddleia davidii, however, is and so are all its varieties, which vary in colour from very dark purple, through shades of lilac, mauve and pink to white. Another excellent white one is Buddleia fallowiana Alba, which has silvery

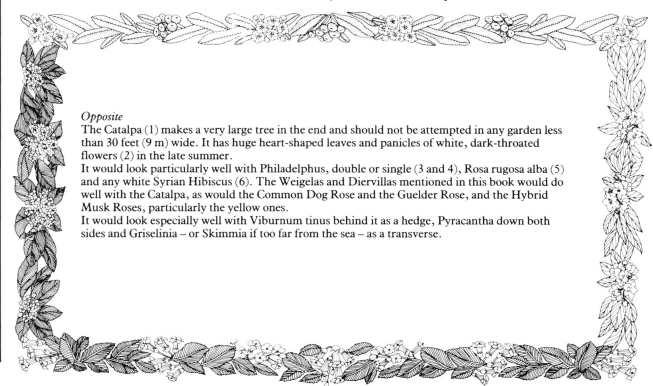

Opposite
The Catalpa (1) makes a very large tree in the end and should not be attempted in any garden less than 30 feet (9 m) wide. It has huge heart-shaped leaves and panicles of white, dark-throated flowers (2) in the late summer.
It would look particularly well with Philadelphus, double or single (3 and 4), Rosa rugosa alba (5) and any white Syrian Hibiscus (6). The Weigelas and Diervillas mentioned in this book would do well with the Catalpa, as would the Common Dog Rose and the Guelder Rose, and the Hybrid Musk Roses, particularly the yellow ones.
It would look especially well with Viburnum tinus behind it as a hedge, Pyracantha down both sides and Griselinia – or Skimmia if too far from the sea – as a transverse.

leaves. Buddleias should be dead-headed in the early autumn and pruned very hard in the spring. They really do attract butterflies.

The Deutzias are nearly all very easy to grow and are beautiful in flower. The French hybrid Deutzia × rosea is perhaps the most satisfying in a small garden, as it is compact but with arching branches – making, indeed, quite a good shape – and has lots of pink, bell-shaped flowers in the summer. There is a very good variety with white flowers, Grandiflora.

The so-called Syrian Hibiscus is hardy in the south of England and in sheltered gardens in the north. It has the great attraction of flowering in the very late summer or early autumn, when all the other shrubs are over. It has many varieties, or hybrids, white, pale pink, red, crimson and blue. It should be allowed to make its own shape as it seems to dislike any really hard pruning; and it must be grown in full sun.

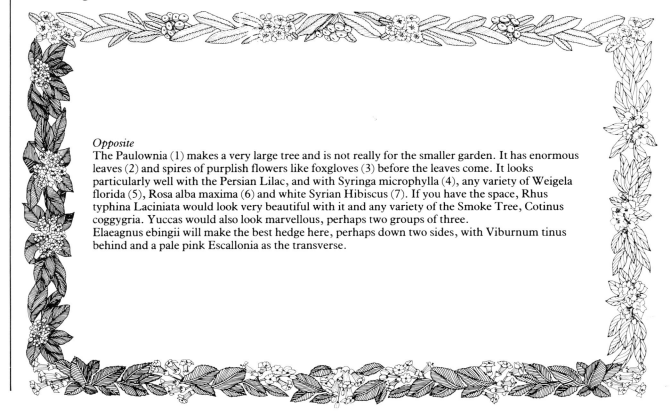

Opposite
The Paulownia (1) makes a very large tree and is not really for the smaller garden. It has enormous leaves (2) and spires of purplish flowers like foxgloves (3) before the leaves come. It looks particularly well with the Persian Lilac, and with Syringa microphylla (4), any variety of Weigela florida (5), Rosa alba maxima (6) and white Syrian Hibiscus (7). If you have the space, Rhus typhina Laciniata would look very beautiful with it and any variety of the Smoke Tree, Cotinus coggygria. Yuccas would also look marvellous, perhaps two groups of three.
Elaeagnus ebingii will make the best hedge here, perhaps down two sides, with Viburnum tinus behind and a pale pink Escallonia as the transverse.

Among the Lilacs, the Persian Lilac (Syringa persica) and a
Chinese lilac (Syringa microphylla) are the best for the small
garden. The former makes a graceful shrub with scented,
lavender-coloured flowers; there is also a white-flowered variety.
The second makes a well-shaped shrub, growing slowly to about
six feet (1.80 m.), with lilac flowers over a long period. These will
give you no trouble and are slightly more subtle than the Common
Lilac (Syringa vulgaris). This can grow very large and, in my view
at least, generally looks rather awkward in the winter.

Still called Syringa by many people, the Mock Orange, or
Philadelphus, has much to offer the One Hour Gardener. Perhaps
the easiest to grow is Philadelphus coronarius, with its golden-
leaved variety Aureus. They can grow very large and should only
be planted where they can do so, because 'keeping them down'
involves cutting off all the growth that would flower the following

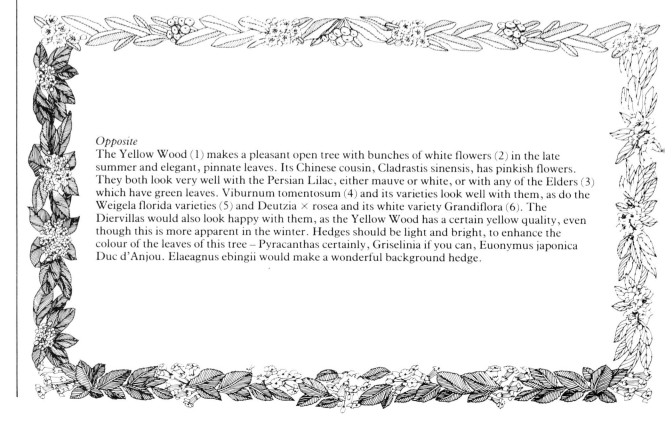

Opposite
The Yellow Wood (1) makes a pleasant open tree with bunches of white flowers (2) in the late
summer and elegant, pinnate leaves. Its Chinese cousin, Cladrastis sinensis, has pinkish flowers.
They both look very well with the Persian Lilac, either mauve or white, or with any of the Elders (3)
which have green leaves. Viburnum tomentosum (4) and its varieties look well with them, as do the
Weigela florida varieties (5) and Deutzia × rosea and its white variety Grandiflora (6). The
Diervillas would also look happy with them, as the Yellow Wood has a certain yellow quality, even
though this is more apparent in the winter. Hedges should be light and bright, to enhance the
colour of the leaves of this tree – Pyracanthas certainly, Griselinia if you can, Euonymus japonica
Duc d'Anjou. Elaeagnus ebingii would make a wonderful background hedge.

year. All have white, or creamy-white, flowers in mid-summer, strongly scented if single. Some of the single varieties have a purple stain at the throat. The double ones are mostly a very pure white. Philadelphus comes in all sizes, from three to fifteen feet (90 cm. to 4.50 m.) and are in all cases easy to grow.

Tree Peonies can be difficult to establish but, on the whole, are worthy of a little patience. It is better not to grow them if your garden is subject to late spring frosts. They like a rich, deep soil neither too acid nor too alkaline. They will positively not grow on thin, chalky soils. In the winter they tend to be ugly but it is possible to regard them as a kind of 'Japanese sculpture'.

They come from Mongolia and Korea, China and Japan. There are many hybrid varieties of Paeonia suffruticosa, pink, crimson, white, carmine and purple. These are the best size for the One Tree Garden and it would be worth discovering a specialist to find the one you want. They are rarely more than four feet (1.20 m.) high.

Paeonia lutea ludlowii and Paeonia delavayi, on the other hand, are two species from Tibet and China which can reach six or five feet (1.80 or 1.50 m.) respectively. They have particularly beautiful leaves, the first with a single yellow flower slightly larger than the crimson flower of the second.

Weigela florida, and its varieties Foliis Purpureis – with purple leaves – and Variegata – with a cream variegation – are easy to grow and handsome, about the right size for the One Tree Garden. There are many garden varieties of Weigela, from crimson through all shades of pink to white. Their flowers are a kind of small trumpet, carried down the whole length of last year's growth, so pruning must be very judicious. It should not, in fact, be necessary at all, if the plants have been sensibly placed.

Not unlike the Weigelas, and frequently confused with them, are the Diervillas. Again, the flowers are like little trumpets carried right up the stem, but they are a beautiful pale yellow. They grow to about five feet (1.50 m.) and are in every way suited to the smaller garden. Diervilla sessilifolia gives good autumn colour. Diervilla × splendens has flowers of a slightly stronger yellow.

Top left

The False Acacia (1) is a very fast growing, graceful tree, tall rather than broad, with great bunches
of white pea-flowers in mid-summer (2) and elegant pinnate leaves.

It looks especially well with the Persian Lilac (3) and with all the Buddleias (4) and with Deutzia ×
rosea Grandiflora (5). Except for coronarius Aureus, all the Philadelphuses will look well with it, as
will Viburnum tomentosum and its varieties, the Common Dog Rose and Rosa alba maxima.
Viburnum tinus would be the best background hedge with Eleagnus ebingii down both sides. The
most charming transverse hedge would be of the Alba Rose Queen of Denmark, or Mme. Legras
de St. Germain, even though they lose their leaves in the winter. Otherwise a pale pink Escallonia
would look extremely well.

Top right

The Pride of India (1) makes an elegant, round-headed tree which has panicles of brilliant yellow
flowers (2) in the late summer and extremely beautiful deeply-cut pinnate leaves. The seeds are
held in curious papery containers. It would look wonderful with the Smoke Tree (3), Cotinus
coggygria or any of its varieties, in front of it. These have purple or purplish leaves and an amazing
feathery flowering that is the reason for the English name. The golden-leaved Elders would look
extremely well with it, as indeed would the green Elders, the larger the better; and all the
Philadelphuses, especially the golden-leaved one, would do so too. All these would require a great
deal of space. In a smaller garden, the Diervillas (4), sessilifolia and splendens, would look
marvellous with it, as would yellow Hybrid Musk Roses. Once more, Viburnum tinus will be the
best background hedge, with Elaeagnus ebingii down one side and Euonymus japonica down the
other. A transverse hedge of yellow Hybrid Musk Roses, Callisto, for instance, or Buff Beauty,
would be the best of all.

Hydrangea paniculata Grandiflora is the Hydrangea that is most at home growing in English grass. It in no way resembles those smug, overweight Hortensias that everyone calls Hydrangeas. It has white flowers which fade to a kind of pink, making a sort of spire like a huge ice cream. They like a rich, damp soil, are rather greedy feeders, and will tolerate a degree of shade, perhaps even prefer it. They will positively not grow on thin soils, either chalky or sooty.

Some 'foliage shrubs' are worth mentioning, mostly because, if you really have room, they look very well with certain of the trees I have mentioned.

Rhus typhina, the Stag's Horn Sumach, and its even more beautiful variety Laciniata, are two of the handsomest 'sculptural' shrubs available to us, both coming from North America. Their flowers are not very interesting, but their autumn colour is splendid and their leaves are at all times a pleasure to look at. They are, of course, deciduous and will make small trees, up to ten feet (3 m.), and they should be so regarded in the One Tree Garden.

Formerly called Rhus cotinus, Cotinus coggygria, its varieties and its relation Cotinus americanus, all offer vivid autumn colour. Some have purple or red leaves all the summer and a hazy, wispy flowering, explaining their old name of Smoke Tree. They can grow to about the same size as Rhus typhina but, being more bushy, can be gently kept down to size which Rhus typhina, on the whole, cannot. Its shape is very important. Perhaps these, too, should be planted as trees in the One Tree Garden.

Should you be on sand, or greensand, then you can grow Camellias and Disanthus cercidifolius. The former, flowering rather unwisely in the very early spring, will tolerate an exactly neutral soil but does not like lime. It grows amazingly well in London, but must be sheltered both from the east wind and the eastern sun. It was suggested for the Absolute Minimum Garden.

Only varieties of Camellia japonica should be attempted by the One Hour Gardener. Its leaves are dark and shiny, a pleasure to look at at all times. Its flowers can be double or single, and vary in colour from purest white through every kind of pink to a clear, clean red. There are one or two rather smart striped ones.

The Disanthus is another 'foliage shrub', according particularly well with trees like the Judas Tree and the Catalpa. Its flowers, which are in fact purple, are so small that they must be searched for; but the autumn colour is well worth waiting for, a glowing wine red, and the leaf shape is always interesting.

Finally, the Yuccas will supply a certain chic to the most uninteresting garden. They make large, dark green rosettes between two and three feet high (60 to 90 cm.), rather tropical looking, and have – though by no means every year and not at all soon – huge spikes of white flowers. Glauca and gloriosa have rigid, very strong-looking leaves; flaccida and recurvifolia, as their names suggest, have a certain suppleness in their leaves. Yucca filamentosa is the most likely to flower when young and they all come from North America.

John Evelyn, in the late seventeenth century, observed that 'the American Yucca is a hardier plant than we take it to be' and suggested that it would make 'the best and most ornamental' hedge in the world. I cannot recommend it as a hedge in a small garden – its points can cause pain to the unwary bender – but as groups growing in grass they would be handsome objects at all times.

Perhaps this is the moment to say, again, that you must not allow your grass to strangle your trees or your shrubs. You do not need to make neatly edged little circles or squares round your plants, as they do in Public Parks; but you do need to keep the point at which your plant emerges from the ground free from other growth. A circle a handspan in diameter should be enough to begin with. Later on, the mature plants will be able to hold their own.

Evergreens in the One Tree Garden

A One Tree Garden composed entirely of evergreens might be a bit overpowering, but you may not think so. I will just say that a mass of heavy evergreens dankly dripping in December is a depressing sight indeed.

The hedges would still be those suggested for the Minimum Garden, preferably those with lighter green leaves, Choisya, Griselinia, Euonymus japonica and Pyracantha. The trees I am about to suggest have nearly all quite dark leaves.

Magnolia grandiflora and Ligustrum lucidum have already been mentioned (on pages 55 and 74 respectively).

The Bay Tree (Laurus nobilis) is a possibility in sheltered conditions in the south. It is inclined to be tender when young and must, in particular, be protected from icy winds. While it is small enough to cover in really severe weather, it should be so covered. When it is too big to cover, it is probably tough enough to withstand the weather. It has phenomenal powers of recovery. Even if it is cut to the ground one winter, don't dig it up; just be patient. As a tree it is pyramidal in shape, rather elegant, and it is most unlikely to exceed twelve feet (3.60 m.).

The Common Holly (Ilex aquifolium) would be an excellent choice for your One Tree. Native, incredibly hardy – though clearly it will make a better tree if sheltered – it makes an upright tree inclined to be narrow. There are good variegated ones, both silver and gold. Only the female tree has berries so, if your neighbour hasn't got one, you may have to include its mate in one of your evergreen hedges. Or plant a holly hedge on the shortest side of your garden as it would be very dominant in a small space.

The Cherry Laurel (Prunus laurocerasus) and the Portugal Laurel (Prunus lusitanica) both make extremely beautiful small trees, their branches sweeping to the ground. The Cherry Laurel has larger leaves than the Portugal and they are somewhat lighter in colour. They both have spikes of white flowers in the late spring, followed by black or dark purple berries not unlike olives. They will stand an ordinary English winter but can be cut to the ground in exceptionally cold ones; after which, like the Bay Tree, they will rise again from the root.

The Strawberry Tree (Arbutus unedo) is a very pretty small tree. It does better within twenty miles (32 km.) of the sea but will grow inland, though not when exposed to north or north-east winds. It

Opposite
The luscious red berries of the Guelder Rose, Viburnum opulus, one of our handsomest native shrubs.

Fatsia japonica (1) makes a small tree, up to ten feet (3 m) only in really good conditions, and is therefore very well suited to the smaller garden. It has magnificent palmate leaves and a strange sort of non-flower (2) in mid-winter. It has immense style and looks as well growing in grass as in paving. It would look particularly well with any of the Mahonias mentioned in this book, Mahonia bealii (3) for instance, though that would give you only winter-flowering shrubs. A large-leaved Escallonia, macrantha (4), would look well with it, or Skimmia japonica (5), particularly if there is a lack of space. Yucca would set it off marvellously, Camellias, the plain green Aucubas and red or yellow Hybrid Musk Roses. I think it better to avoid large white flowers with Fatsia, although Hebe salicifolia, with dozens of white bottle-brush flowers and slender apple-green leaves would set it off very well.

The hedges should be light and bright, Griselinia if you can, Euonymus japonica in variety, Elaeagnus ebingii, Pyracantha; Choisya would make an excellent transverse hedge.

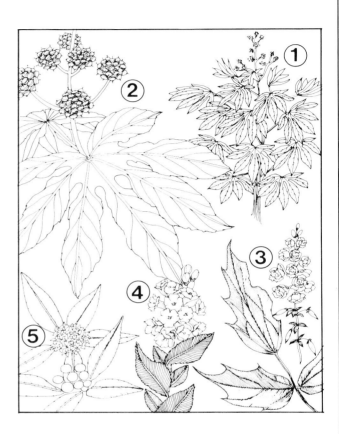

has a small, transparent, bell-like flower and a strawberry-like fruit, both on the tree together in the autumn. There is one with pink flowers, Arbutus unedo Rubra, and they are very unlikely to top ten feet (3 m.).

Fatsia japonica is a most obliging plant frequently, and mistakenly, called the Castor Oil Plant. I dread to think what would happen if you took any oil that could be squeezed out of a Fatsia. It has huge shiny leaves, larger than one's hand and, like one's hand, 'palmate'. It has a strange white inflorescence – one cannot really call it a flower – in mid-winter and will grow in the most unlikely situations, particularly in towns. In good conditions it will make a large shrub, or small tree, up to ten feet (3 m.), always interesting to look at.

Opposite
Cornus alba Elegantissima looks its best against dark or light green, but does not consort well with yellow, or golden-variegated, leaves.

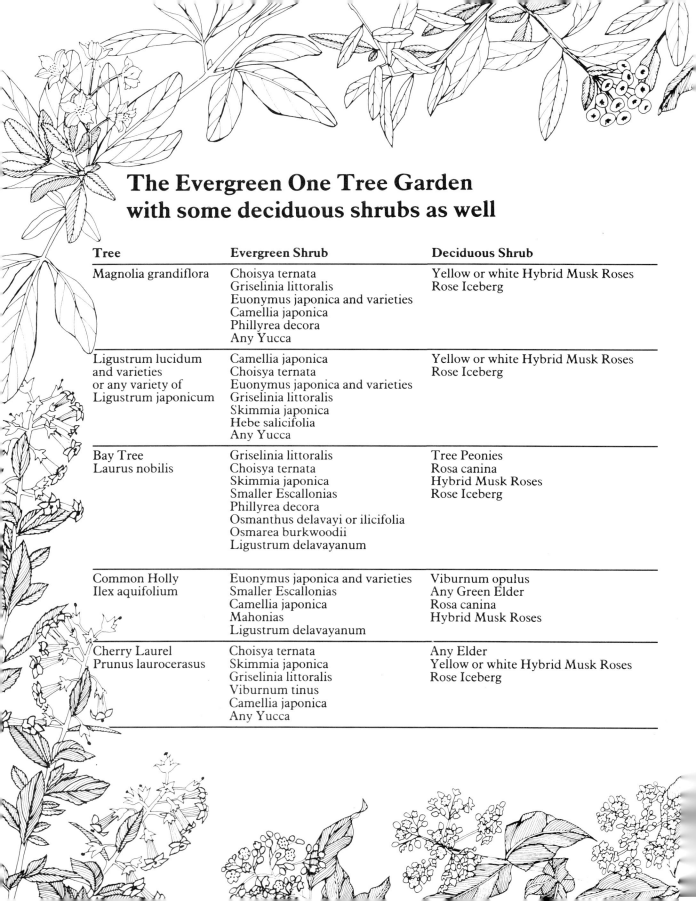

The Evergreen One Tree Garden
with some deciduous shrubs as well

Tree	Evergreen Shrub	Deciduous Shrub
Magnolia grandiflora	Choisya ternata Griselinia littoralis Euonymus japonica and varieties Camellia japonica Phillyrea decora Any Yucca	Yellow or white Hybrid Musk Roses Rose Iceberg
Ligustrum lucidum and varieties or any variety of Ligustrum japonicum	Camellia japonica Choisya ternata Euonymus japonica and varieties Griselinia littoralis Skimmia japonica Hebe salicifolia Any Yucca	Yellow or white Hybrid Musk Roses Rose Iceberg
Bay Tree Laurus nobilis	Griselinia littoralis Choisya ternata Skimmia japonica Smaller Escallonias Phillyrea decora Osmanthus delavayi or ilicifolia Osmarea burkwoodii Ligustrum delavayanum	Tree Peonies Rosa canina Hybrid Musk Roses Rose Iceberg
Common Holly Ilex aquifolium	Euonymus japonica and varieties Smaller Escallonias Camellia japonica Mahonias Ligustrum delavayanum	Viburnum opulus Any Green Elder Rosa canina Hybrid Musk Roses
Cherry Laurel Prunus laurocerasus	Choisya ternata Skimmia japonica Griselinia littoralis Viburnum tinus Camellia japonica Any Yucca	Any Elder Yellow or white Hybrid Musk Roses Rose Iceberg

Portugal Laurel Prunus lusitanica	Any Escallonia Phillyrea decora Osmanthus delavayi or ilicifolia Osmarea burkwoodii Choisya ternata Griselinia littoralis Mahonias Ligustrum delavayanum	Cornus alba Variegata Cornus alba sibirica Variegata Cornus mas Variegata Cornus alternifolia Argentea Hybrid Musk Roses Rose Iceberg

Strawberry Tree
Arbutus unedo
Arbutus unedo Rubra
	Osmanthus delavayi or ilicifolia
	Phillyrea decora
	Any Escallonia
	Griselinia littoralis
	Hebe salicifolia
	Skimmia japonica
		Hybrid Musk Roses
		Rose Iceberg
		Medium-sized Philadelphus
		with Rubra: Dog Rose
		          Deutzia x rosea
		          Weigela florida and varieties

Pittosporum tenuifolium	Euonymus japonica Duc d'Anjou Griselinia littoralis Choisya ternata Skimmia japonica Osmanthus delavayi or ilicifolia Osmarea burkwoodii Phillyrea decora Aucuba Longifolia m and f Hebe salicifolia Any Escallonia Ligustrum delavayanum	Tree Peonies Hybrid Musk Roses Rose Iceberg
Fatsia japonica	Choisya ternata Griselinia littoralis Hebe salicifolia Euonymus japonica species and Duc d'anjou Camellia japonica Escallonia macrantha Skimmia japonica Aucuba Longifolia m and f Mahonias Any Yucca	Hybrid Musk Roses Tree Peonies

The Evergreen Hedges are those suggested for the Minimum Garden. Choose your tree and one shrub only, planting two of it, and one of something else only if you are sure you have room.

Finally, Pittosporum tenuifolium, from New Zealand, will make a charming small tree in the southern counties, and up the west coast, of Great Britain. It has small twisting leaves – probably you have had some sent to you with Florist's Flowers and wondered what it was – and flowers, on the mature plant, in late spring. It would look particularly well in company with its compatriot, Griselinia littoralis. It is hardier than one thinks and also makes an excellent hedge.

Existing Trees in the One Tree Garden

Hitherto it has been assumed that there was an empty garden to start from, but this in fact is not very usual in England. More likely you are faced with one tree in a very odd position, so that the game now is to make it look as if it were intended to be there.

In some ways the kind of solution suggested for Trees in the Minimum Garden (figures 5 & 6) is the easiest, that is to say containing your tree in a shape made by hedges; but this only works well if your garden is much longer than it is wide. If it is more of a fat rectangle, then you may have to place your tree in a shape of longer grass.

The circle and the square are quite the easiest shapes to achieve on the ground, and quite the most satisfactory to look at. But the double square – twice as long as it is wide – is also an excellent shape, as are rectangles three, four or five times longer than they are wide.

Try to make such a shape with your tree in it, leaving at least one width of the mower between your hedges and the longer grass. Doing that, in fact, may be a very good point from which to start. Then you plant the bulbs and shrubs that *you* want and try to achieve a balanced composition.

Symmetry can be achieved in a small garden – not, of course, if you already have one tree – but I am not sure that it is really desirable, being curiously tiring on a small scale. Balance is more subtle – and more difficult to achieve – but in a small garden is the more satisfying in the end.

Figure 12
Plan of a One Tree Garden, with an existing tree, in this case a kind of Maple. A rectangle of longer grass, five times as long as it is wide, has been made with the tree at the end of it. The tree is now balanced by three shrubs, in this case Guelder Rose.

A large shrub will balance an existing small tree – when it is fully grown, I must hasten to add. A group of three small shrubs will balance a large shrub. Three large shrubs will balance a larger tree, and so on. It is usually easier to place an odd number of shrubs than an even one.

In figure 12 the tree now finds itself at the end of a long rectangle of longer grass, which occupies about a third of the width of the garden. Shrubs have been planted in it and the fact that the 'composition' exists on one side of the garden only does not matter, as it is balanced by the hedge on the other side.

Even if you have excellent walls, or fences, the plants that grow up them tend to need a lot of looking after, and mostly look rather depressing in the winter. Hedges are a vital constituent of the One Hour Garden, because they offer a very strong framework able to contain almost anything, hopeless muddles or displays of genius. As your shape is being made by you and your mower it can of course be easily altered; but not after you have planted your bulbs.

A few more Evergreen Shrubs

Skimmia japonica, Camellia japonica and Euonymus japonica have all been mentioned in connection with Minimum Gardens. They will also be useful here. There are three varieties of the Euonymus which make handsomer shrubs than the species: the Duc d'Anjou, very interesting in two shades of green; Macrophylla Alba, with a broad, white-margined leaf; and Albo-marginata, with a narrow white-margined leaf.

The Aucubas (Spotty Laurel), also from Japan, are a much misunderstood race. Extensively planted in towns in the nineteenth century, as they are peculiarly smoke-resistant, they have received a very bad press ever since. So far as there is such a thing as a foolproof evergreen shrub, you will find it here.

The unvariegated ones are, I think, handsomer than the better known variegated ones and they look particularly well when the female plant is in berry. You must therefore have two to get any berries and the best are probably: Crassifolia, male; Hillieri, female; Longifolia, male and female, and Salicifolia, female. Perhaps, in a small garden, two Longifolia would be best.

It is almost impossible to kill an Aucuba and it responds particularly well to kindness.

Osmanthus ilicifolia and delavayi, Phillyrea angustifolia and Osmarea burkwoodii have all been mentioned in the Minimum Garden. Grown free, they all make handsome shrubs which can be discreetly cut back if they get too large. Phillyrea decora makes an even better shrub than angustifolia.

The winter-flowering Mahonias are all very spectacular. They all have quite large compound leaves, with holly-like leaflets – in other words they are prickly – and yellow flowers like bunches of lily-of-the-valley, sometimes strongly scented. The best ones are Mahonia bealei, Mahonia japonica, Mahonia pinnata and the tender, and magnificent, Mahonia lomarifolia. Mahonia pinnata can grow to eight feet (2.40 m.), but the others are usually between four and six feet (1.20 to 1.80 m).

Finally, Hebe salicifolia has a beautiful pale, apple green leaf which would contrast well with the dark trees. It is entirely covered in the summer with white bottle-brush flowers. It can grow up to ten feet (3 metres) but is usually nearer six (1.80 m.). It will withstand the usual winters in England, but can be carried off in a really severe one.

There is a fairly general feeling in England that plants should be available free, like books from the library. None of the plants mentioned here will be found to be very cheap, in particular those to be used as hedges will not be available at the hedging rate. But it is important to remember that the first planting should be the only planting. Thereafter, except for disasters, which do happen, your plants should merely increase in size and beauty every year, while you beam at them from your deck chair.

On pages 92-93 there is a table of suggested combinations of trees and shrubs in the Evergreen One Tree Garden.

THE TWO TREE GARDEN

Two Tree Gardens are rather difficult. If you have room for only two trees, as opposed to three, it is important to position them as asymmetrically as possible. If you are using circles or squares it is equally important that they should *obviously* be of different sizes.

At figure 13 is a plan of a Two Tree Garden as it might be planted from scratch. A small tree is planted at the end of a double square of longer grass, with a larger tree in a circle in the top right hand corner. The trees should be different but, ideally, should have the same kind of leaf, that is to say pinnate or heart-shaped. In this case the tree on the left might be a Rowan, or Mountain Ash, and the larger one a Manna Ash; or a Judas Tree and an Idesia. But this, of course, is not always possible and on pages 104 and 105 will be found some suggestions for suitable pairs.

More probably, however, you already have your two trees. If they have been planted as a pair then the plan at figure 14 might help you. More usually, though, they will have been planted without any particular thought and you must try to give them a sort of logic by the placing of your shapes. At figures 15, 16 and 17 are some suggestions that may be helpful.

Should you have some trees placed as they are in figure 17, my instinct would be to remove the one in the bottom right hand corner. It would, of course, depend on what it was and, should you live in a conservation area, it would probably not be allowed.

The trees are very unlikely to be any of those I have suggested. If you have Japanese Cherries then you can associate them with any shrub that has the suffix 'japonica', thus creating what is called, in solemn circles, 'an ecological grouping'. The result may be a bit bizarre but it will not be dull.

The Flowering Crabs, or any member of the Prunus family – except laurocerasus and lusitanica – should be treated as Fruit Trees for association purposes. You could consult the list for Cherry, Plum or Quince under the One Tree Garden. Heavy conifers should be treated as Bay or Holly in the previous Evergreen list.

Figure 13
Plan of a Two Tree Garden, planted from scratch. The tree in the circle is a Manna Ash, accompanied by one Weigela; the one in the double square is a Mountain Ash, accompanied by two Tree Peonies.

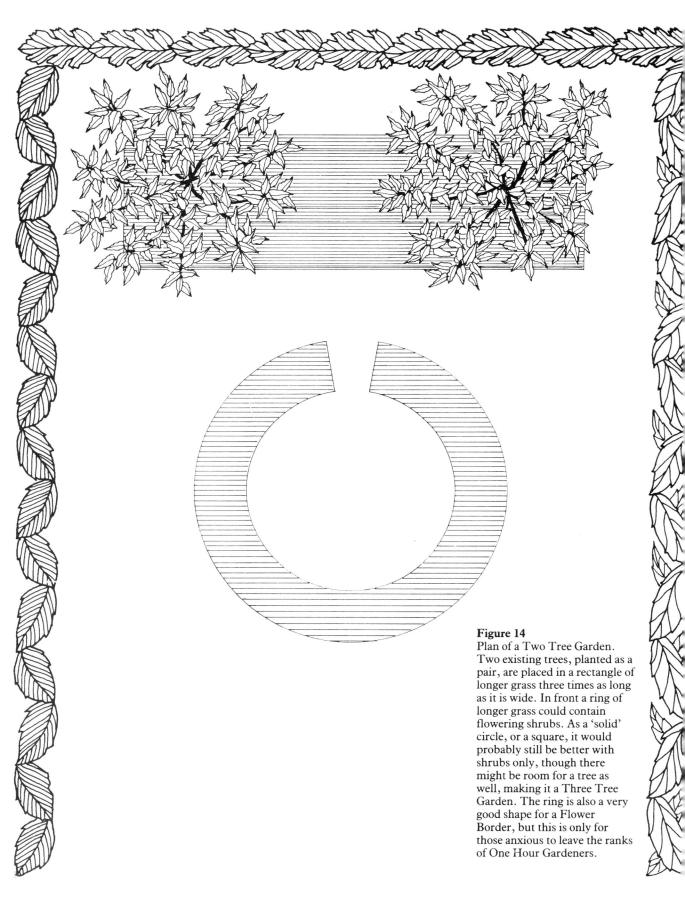

Figure 14
Plan of a Two Tree Garden.
Two existing trees, planted as a
pair, are placed in a rectangle of
longer grass three times as long
as it is wide. In front a ring of
longer grass could contain
flowering shrubs. As a 'solid'
circle, or a square, it would
probably still be better with
shrubs only, though there
might be room for a tree as
well, making it a Three Tree
Garden. The ring is also a very
good shape for a Flower
Border, but this is only for
those anxious to leave the ranks
of One Hour Gardeners.

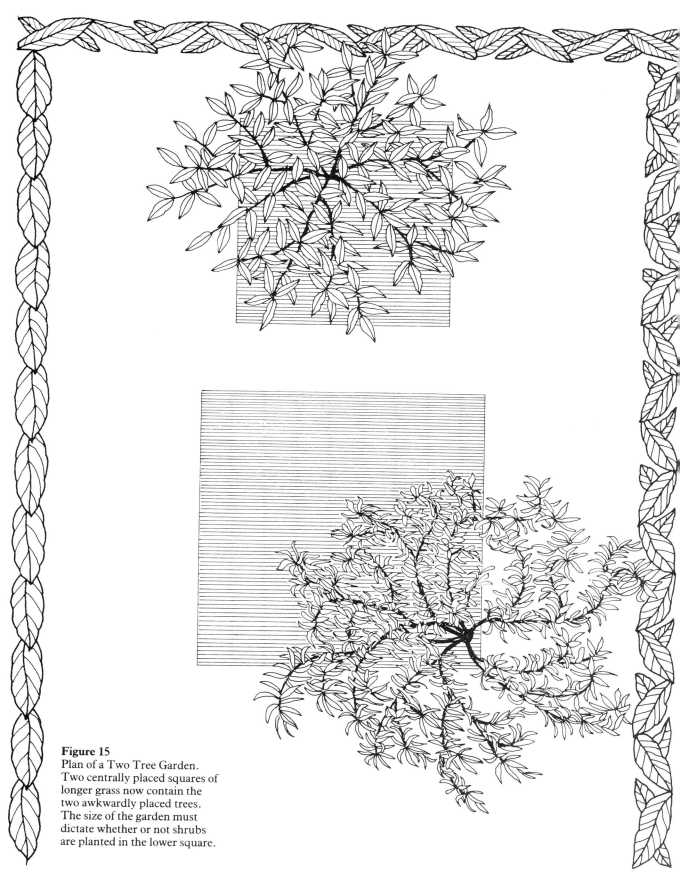

Figure 15
Plan of a Two Tree Garden.
Two centrally placed squares of
longer grass now contain the
two awkwardly placed trees.
The size of the garden must
dictate whether or not shrubs
are planted in the lower square.

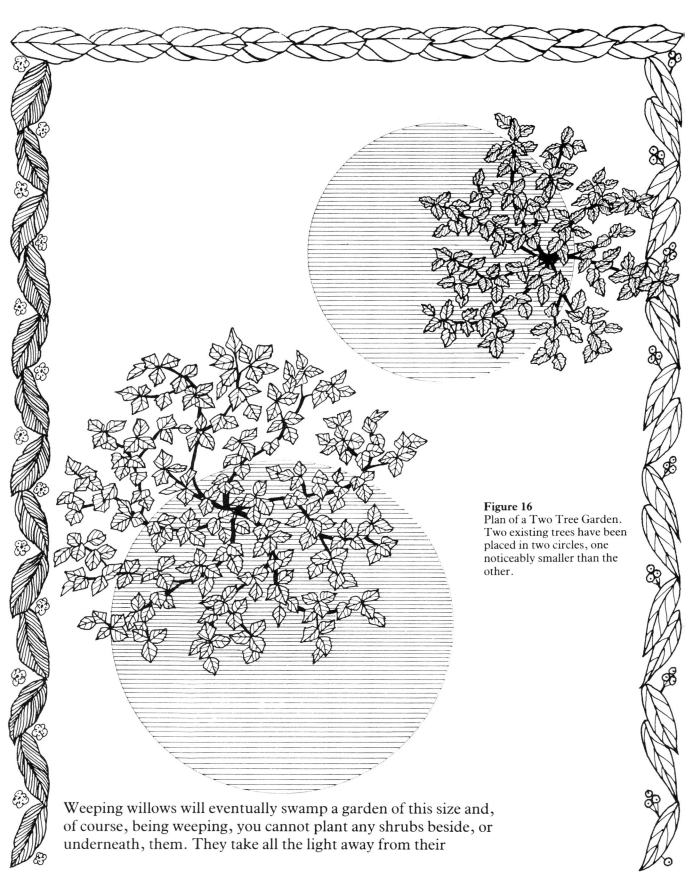

Figure 16
Plan of a Two Tree Garden.
Two existing trees have been
placed in two circles, one
noticeably smaller than the
other.

Weeping willows will eventually swamp a garden of this size and,
of course, being weeping, you cannot plant any shrubs beside, or
underneath, them. They take all the light away from their

neighbours. If you have room for a second grass shape then a very large shrub, or very small tree, can be planted in it. In this precise case, Rhus typhina or Rhus typhina Laciniata would look extremely well, or Sorbaria arborea.

If it has to be grown alone, then emphasise it by placing it in a large grass shape planted only with bulbs. Even as young trees they look better by themselves. I have not suggested them, beautiful though they can be, because they are too large for gardens of this size. They are really at their best planted in conjunction with pieces of water considerably larger than themselves.

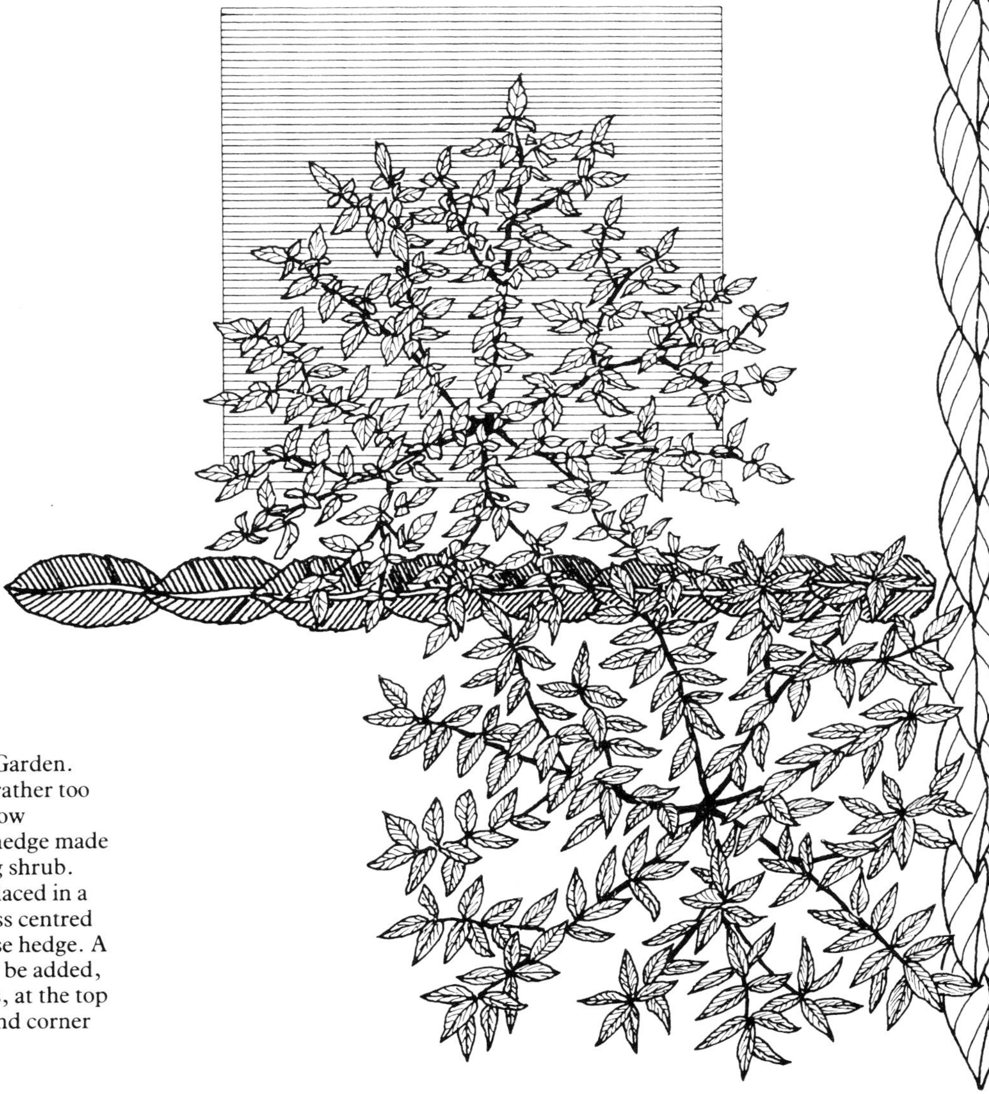

Figure 17
Plan of a Two Tree Garden.
Two existing trees, rather too close together, are now separated by a new hedge made of any shade-bearing shrub. The farther tree is placed in a square of longer grass centred on the new transverse hedge. A third tree could well be added, standing in cut grass, at the top left, or top right, hand corner of this garden.

Suggested Pairs for the Two Tree Garden

The larger tree is given first. The Whitebeam, the Snowdrop Tree and the False Acacia may eventually make heads as much as 20 feet through (6 m.). The others will be between 12 and 15 feet (3.60 and 4.50 m.), if as much.

Manna Ash	*with*	Weigela florida Venusta (or other pink)
Mountain Ash	*with*	Paeonia lutea ludlowii
Idesia polycarpa	*with*	Hydrangea paniculata Grandiflora
Judas Tree	*with*	Diervilla sessilifolia
Whitebeam	*with*	Wayfaring Tree
Cockspur Thorn	*with*	Guelder Rose
Snowdrop Tree	*with*	Viburnum tomentosum
Bird Cherry	*with*	Syringa persica Alba
Fig Tree	*with*	Red Elder
Chinese Angelica Tree	*with*	Weigela florida Mont Blanc
Snowdrop Tree	*with*	Syringa persica Alba
Cockspur Thorn	*with*	Hibiscus syriacus Snowdrift (white)
False Acacia	*with*	Philadelphus coronarius
Mountain Ash	*with*	Syringa persica Alba
Gingko biloba	*with*	Hibiscus syriacus Duc de Brabant (double red) or Rubis (single red)
Eucryphia glutinosa	*with*	Diervilla sessilifolia
False Acacia	*with*	American Elder
Manna Ash	*with*	Hydrangea paniculata Grandiflora
Idesia polycarpa	*with*	Hybrid Musk Rose Prosperity (white)
Fig Tree	*with*	Paeonia suffruticosa Hybrid
Whitebeam	*with*	White Rose of York, Rosa alba maxima
Bird Cherry	*with*	Wayfaring Tree
Sorbaria arborea	*with*	American Elder
Chinese Angelica Tree	*with*	Buddleia davidii White Cloud
Judas Tree	*with*	Viburnum tomentosum
Fig Tree	*with*	Yucca filamentosa (or other Yucca)
Cockspur Thorn	*with*	Guelder Rose
Mountain Ash	*with*	Californian Elder
Gingko biloba	*with*	Yucca filamentosa (or other Yucca)
Fig Tree	*with*	Viburnum tomentosum
Gingko biloba	*with*	Diervilla sessilifolia
Chinese Angelica Tree	*with*	Hydrangea paniculata Grandiflora
Gingko biloba	*with*	Sambucus canadensis maxima
Sorbaria arborea	*with*	Yucca filamentosa (or other Yucca)
Euodia hupehensis	*with*	Weigela florida Mont Blanc
Manna Ash	*with*	Diervilla sessilifolia
Amur Cork Tree	*with*	Hydrangea paniculata Grandiflora
Mountain Ash	*with*	Red Elder
False Acacia	*with*	Viburnum tomentosum
Amur Cork Tree	*with*	Deutzia x rosea Grandiflora (white)
Euodia hupehensis	*with*	Californian Elder
Cockspur Thorn	*with*	Guelder Rose

For Larger Gardens

The larger tree is given first. Catalpas and Paulownias may eventually make a head of 30 feet (9 m.) through, but this will take rather more than thirty years. The others may be thought of as achieving between 15 and 20 feet (4.50 m. and 6 m.) through, at the most.

A Catalpa	*with*	Guelder Rose
Magnolia sinensis	*with*	Wayfaring Tree
A Paulownia	*with*	Syringa persica Alba
Idesia polycarpa	*with*	Guelder Rose
Yellow Wood	*with*	Buddleia davidii White Bouquet
Manna Ash	*with*	Red Elder
Handkerchief Tree	*with*	Rosa rugosa alba
Golden Rain Tree	*with*	Diervilla sessilifolia
A Catalpa	*with*	Hybrid Musk Prosperity (white)
Idesia polycarpa	*with*	Rose Iceberg
A Paulownia	*with*	Diervilla sessilifolia
A large-leaved Magnolia	*with*	Weigela florida Venusta (or other pink)
Yellow Wood	*with*	Hibiscus syriacus Monstrosus (white)
False Acacia	*with*	Paeonia suffruticosa Hybrid
False Acacia	*with*	Philadelphus coronarius
Gleditschia triacanthos Inermis	*with*	Guelder Rose
Handkerchief Tree	*with*	Hydrangea paniculata Grandiflora
Idesia polycarpa	*with*	Weigela florida Venusta (or other pink)
Golden Rain Tree	*with*	Hibiscus syriacus Totus Albus or Snowdrift
Sorbaria arborea	*with*	Buddleia davidii Black Night
Yellow Wood	*with*	Buddleia davidii White Bouquet
Sorbaria arborea	*with*	Buddleia davidii Black Night
Golden Rain Tree	*with*	Sambucus canadensis Aurea
Manna Ash	*with*	Philadelphus coronarius Aureus (two golden-leaved shrubs)

All with golden leaves:

Robinia Frisia	*with*	Philadelphus coronarius Aureus
Gleditschia triacanthos Sunburst	*with*	Sambucus racemosa Plumosa Aurea

Golden leaves and golden variegations:

Acer negundo Auratum	*with*	Sambucus nigra Aureo-marginata
Acer negundo Elegantissimum	*with*	Sambucus racemosa Plumosa Aurea

In a very wide garden only:

A Catalpa	*with*	Philadelphus coronarius
A Paulownia	*with*	Sambucus canadensis maxima
Amur Cork Tree	*with*	Sambucus canadensis maxima
Euodia hupehensis	*with*	Any Tree Peony
Euodia hupehensis	*with*	Hybrid Musk Rose Prosperity
Amur Cork Tree	*with*	Rose Iceberg

These are the decorative trees. Any two fruit trees will look well with one another. For their associated shrubs, consult the suggestions for the One Tree Garden. In a small garden you will be better to choose, for instance, two Roses, or two Philadelphus, or two Viburnums, two Buddleias, etc.

AWKWARD ANGLES AND LUMPY GARDENS

Hitherto it has been assumed that your garden is a straightforward rectangle and, if yours is a newly-built house, that is likely to be the case. It has also been supposed that the garden is behind the house – that is to say that the house is, in all the previous plans, at the bottom of the page. This, however, is unfortunately by no means always the case, particularly not if your house is more than fifty years old.

If your house has garden on both sides of it, and also at the front, as in figure 18, then you must section it off, in your own mind at least, and think of it as two, or three, One or Two Tree Gardens.

In this case, the piece of grass at the bottom of the plan is too narrow to contain anything but one tree and the grass here should be kept short. The space between the drive to the garage and the path to the front door is large enough to contain a circle of longer grass – it is too awkward a shape to contain a square – with some bulbs and low-growing shrubs in it; while the lawn beyond, an extremely peculiar shape when considered alone, is large enough to contain two circles placed, if not exactly at random, at least irregularly.

As before, hedges surround the garden, but here you must be careful in your choice as some of them, notably in the little bit below the garage on the plan, are going to have very little sun.

Circles are unquestionably the best way to induce harmony among a number of unhelpful angles, as they will 'float' anywhere. In general it will be wise to make them of noticeably different sizes, as in figure 20, and not to attempt to centralise any of them.

In this case the garden is an unhappy quadrilateral and it does not have a central axis. None of the corners is a right-angle, so that the hedges may make ugly angles when they meet. In this case, therefore, it will be better to choose hedges that do not contrast too sharply with each other. But the outline shape of the garden must be accepted, though the attention is to be diverted from it. This can be done by using three different circles, as in figure 20, or one large one, as in figure 19.

Opposite
The wonderful spires of Yucca gloriosa, unfortunately only produced on mature plants.

Overleaf
Arbutus unedo Rubra, the pink-flowered Strawberry Tree, makes a small, very elegant, evergreen tree.

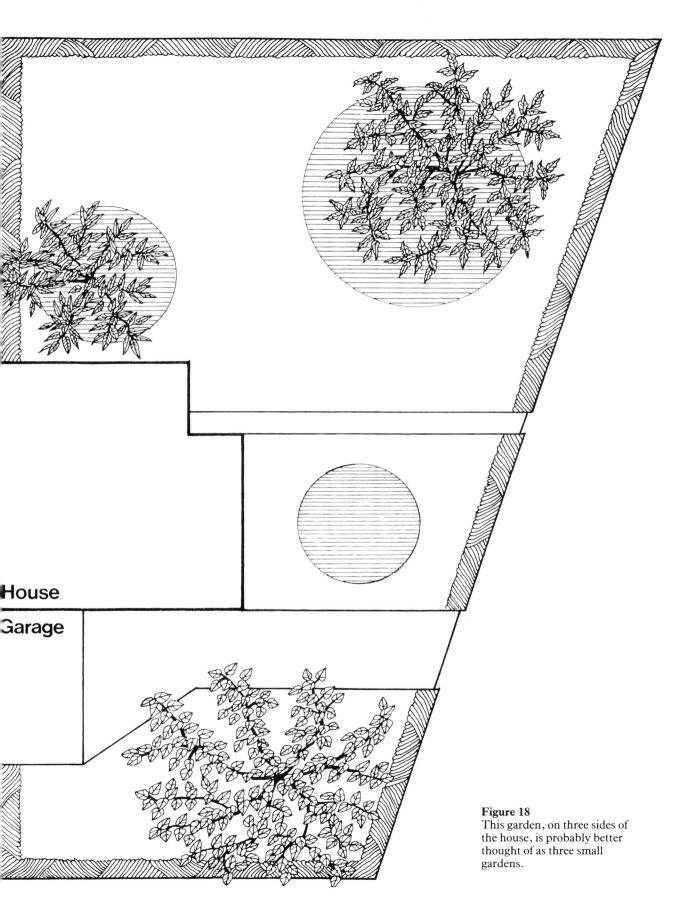

Figure 18
This garden, on three sides of the house, is probably better thought of as three small gardens.

Figure 19
One large circle pulls the three
sides of this garden together. A
tree conceals the awkward
corner.

By planting the circles with trees and shrubs and bulbs as previously suggested, the attention is focused away from the awkward corners and the shape of the garden begins to work for you instead of against you. In particular, by planting a tree towards the sharp corner at the top right hand corner of the garden, you will eventually make that awkward angle 'disappear'.

There is no place for a transverse hedge in this garden, as they are only successful when making a right-angle with a wall or another hedge. Similarly, squares are of no use here as two sides of any square must always be parallel to two sides of the garden, or one side of the garden and a transverse hedge at right-angles to it.

L-shaped gardens are another likelihood, and these are most easily dealt with by making two distinct rectangles out of the L, as in figure 21. In this case, the top part of the garden could be maintained as it were separately, as an orchard or a children's garden, leaving a grass path one or two widths of the mower all the way round.

In all these cases, it is important that the trees should harmonise with each other and the simplest way to ensure this is to choose trees which have a similar leaf shape. For our purposes, the trees suggested in this book have four leaf shapes: pinnate, like the Mountain Ash; cordate, or heart-shaped, like the Catalpa; palmate, like the Fig or the Fatsia. The others have leaves best described as 'simple', as one might say 'leaf-shaped', like the Apple and the Whitebeam. These are the bases of the association tables on pages 104 and 105, and 122 and 123, though clearly not every pair, or trio, of harmonising trees will have similarly shaped leaves.

A Palmate leaf

A Cordate leaf

A Pinnate leaf

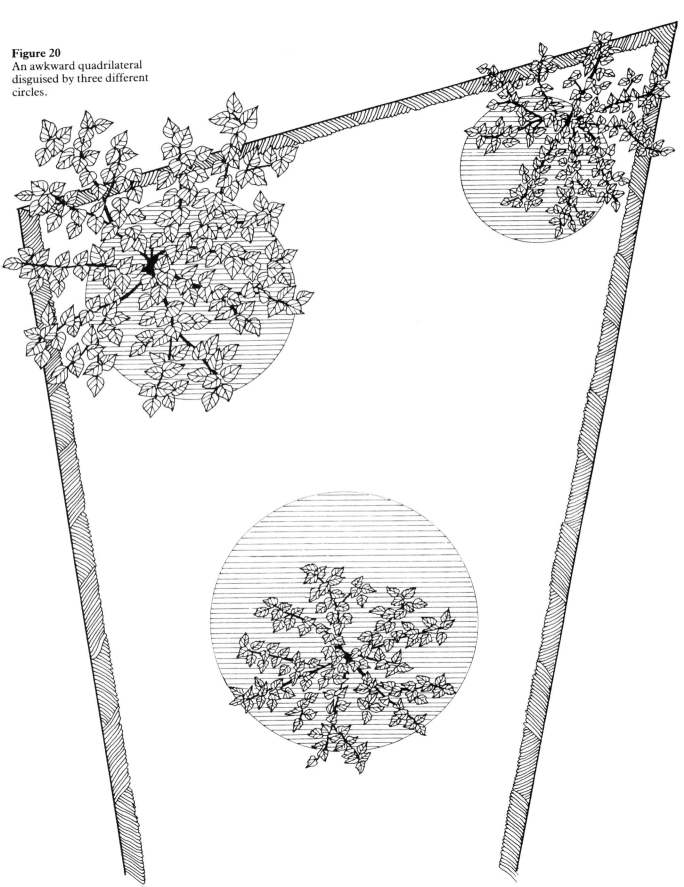

Figure 20
An awkward quadrilateral
disguised by three different
circles.

As I have said, the circle and the square are the easiest shapes to achieve on the ground and they can be used, alone or together, to furnish the most awkward outline shapes. 'Free-form' gardening is better left to the few great artists who can do it well. Sir William Temple, a noted gardener at the end of the seventeenth century, regarded 'irregular' gardening as extremely difficult, 'whereas in regular figures it is hard to make any great and remarkable faults.' Unless your garden is naturally contoured – in which case you have only to follow the contours – it is probably wiser to stick to the square, the double square and the circle for your shapes of longer grass.

So often free-form gardens consist of what appear to be random jig-saw puzzle pieces, in the form of little ponds or flower beds or shrubberies or just pieces of grass, which do not fit together, and which give an effect at once disturbing and artificial, although the *intention* is to give a natural effect. Probably we have all been told that the straight line does not exist in Nature, any more than the circle does. This, however, is not a reason for not using them in urban or suburban surroundings and particularly not when the boundary lines of the garden are, in fact, straight, forming a recognisable geometrical shape, whether square, rectangle, quadrilateral or irregular pentagon.

Do not be afraid of emphasising the shape of your garden by planting its boundaries with hedges. There is almost no shape that you are likely to encounter that cannot be rendered agreeable, or at any rate bearable, by judiciously placed circles of longer grass, with their attendant trees.

Symmetry is really only successful on a very large scale and it should certainly not be attempted here. In a small garden any feature, such as a path or hedge, dividing the garden down the centre will make that garden look smaller; it will convert it into two strips. In a small garden shaped like the one at figures 19 and 20 any attempt to give the garden a 'spine' – as by a broad grass path centred on the house – would merely serve to emphasise the differences between the two halves thus created. At figure 27 this has in fact been done, but the garden under consideration there is at least ten times the size of the one at figures 19 and 20.

Figure 21
An L-shaped garden divided into a One Tree Garden and a Two Tree Garden.

The gardens so far have all been small, and flat. If they are not exactly flat then the chances are that the slope will be gentle enough to make it possible to plant them as though they were. Really hilly gardens are perhaps beyond the scope of this book, but it could be said that the geometrical shapes so far recommended will be of less use in them. Probably the contours of the garden will give the shapes, naturally and gracefully.

Plant the 'hills', or banks, with shrubs and trees and leave them in longer grass to be cut only three or four times a year. Leave the 'valleys', or flatter parts, clear and maintain them as lawn. You should then have a garden that is logical and elegant. If a tree should occur in your lawn, then leave it there of course, as trees look quite sensible growing in short grass. Shrubs, however, do not and these should be firmly moved to the lumpier parts of your garden.

THE THREE TREE GARDEN

For a garden this size you will certainly require a brush and a rake, a wheelbarrow and, unless your dustmen are unusually accommodating, somewhere to put your grass cuttings. These can be used, while your hedges are young, as a mulch – that is to say, a covering for the bare earth between your hedging shrubs, keeping the weeds down and the moisture in.

When your mulch has rotted – it is wise to turn it over with a fork from time to time – then it can be dug in. Unless your distances are very long, a long-handled handfork is adequate for this. Otherwise a light digging fork, sometimes known as a Ladies' Fork, will do this very well.

When your hedges are mature, however, this will be impossible and you may be obliged to disguise your cuttings as kitchen refuse and put them in the dustbin. On the other hand, if you plant the hedge at the top of your garden about three feet (90 cm.) away from your boundary wall, or fence (figures 22-25), you will have room for a small incinerator (for burning leaves) and a compost heap (which your Keen Gardener friends will take away from you every two years, in sacks).

The Three Tree Garden is in fact quite large, the garden at least of a semi-detached house. In general, the smaller trees on the previous lists will have a head, when fully grown, between twelve and fifteen feet across (3.60 to 4.50 m.) and it is probably better if they do not meet. The minimum size for this garden, therefore, is twenty-five by fifty feet, or seven-and-a-half by fifteen metres. At this minimum size, you would do better to plant the trees without the shrubs.

As in the Two Tree Garden, you contain your three trees in shapes that are related to one another. In a larger garden, you can mix circles and squares (figure 22) which may be more convenient if you already have one or two of your three trees. The hedges are still those from the Minimum Garden and the trees any of those previously mentioned, with their associated shrubs.

Figure 22
A Three Tree Garden with a Square, a Circle and a Strip in the proportion of 1:5. The trees are, top to bottom, a Catalpa with a Hybrid Musk Rose; a Paulownia with Rosa alba maxima; and an Idesia or a Mulberry with the Common Dog Rose.

Some Hedges for Larger Gardens

You may, however, have a much larger garden than the minimum size, big enough for you to consider hedges which would be, on the whole, too overpowering in a smaller space.

First among these must be the three native evergreens, the Yew (Taxus baccata), the Box Tree (Buxus sempervirens) and the Common Holly (Ilex aquifolium). The first and third of these can probably be obtained at Hedging Rate from good nurserymen. All three have the inestimable advantage of growing facing the north, but they will do so very slowly. These are not hedges for the middle-aged, or for anyone in a hurry.

On the other hand, in time, they make beautiful, close hedges almost entirely indestructible and practically impenetrable. They are gloomy grown in a small space – except possibly the Holly – and not quite interesting enough to be grown as the sole occupants of a garden, which is why they were not suggested for the Minimum Garden.

Holly grows slightly faster than Yew and much faster than Box. It has many interesting varieties. It is also sexed, but in any length of hedge you would be bound to have a mixture of the two. There are smooth-leaved hollies, golden-variegated, silver-variegated, extra prickly and quite prickly. Some, notably Hodgin's Holly, a great favourite in the last century, are only male and therefore will not berry. All make excellent hedges and the berrying kinds will produce their berries even when closely clipped.

The Yew is more sombre, but a superb background hedge, particularly to variegated and shiny-leaved shrubs. It grows in fact much faster than its publicity suggests and it will thrive even on not very good chalky soils. It doesn't seem to like a heavy clay very much. Its leaves are poisonous to cattle and its berries – it is very unlikely to have any as a properly maintained hedge – are poisonous to people.

The planting of a Box hedge would be to make a real gesture towards the future, though it is in some ways the handsomest of the three. It has several varieties and the smell of its leaves in hot sun is disliked by some people. There are also several kinds of Dwarf Box – ordinarily sold as 'Box Edging' – and this will not do for you at all.

Figure 23
Plan of a Three Tree Garden. A square and two strips – one in the proportion of 4 to 1, the other of 5 to 1 – contain the trees and their attendant shrubs. Top to bottom: a Catalpa and two Rose Bushes; a Fig Tree and an Elder Bush; a Judas Tree and a Disanthus (only suitable for acid soils).

Three deciduous native trees, the Lime (Tilia platyphyllos), the Beech (Fagus sylvatica), and the Hornbeam (Carpinus betulus), also make excellent hedges, but again only in relatively large spaces. They are most effective as long, high hedges seen from a distance and are not really suitable for the average urban, or suburban, garden.

There are Beeches with coloured leaves, but I am inclined to think that Purple or Copper Beeches make a gloomy hedge. The golden-leaved Fagus sylvatica Zlatia, however, would make a ravishing, and extremely expensive, hedge, a particularly good background to evergreens.

Beech also grows very well on alkaline soils. If your soil is inclined to be heavy, the Hornbeam will do better.

Three evergreen foreigners should be noticed here. Rhamnus alaternus, already mentioned for the Absolute Minimum Garden, is the Alaternus of John Evelyn, the seventeenth-century writer who first used the Yew as a hedge. Curiously, it looks well either on a very small, or on a very large, scale.

The Holm Oak (Quercus ilex) makes a most beautiful hedge with a faint look of olive trees about it; and Pittosporum tenuifolium, already mentioned as an evergreen tree for sheltered places, makes a superb hedge, also in sheltered places. They are only suitable for really large gardens and I should perhaps mention that, on any suitable scale, they would cost a great deal of money.

The permutations are by this time enormous. In general, I think the trees should be chosen first. Very probably the choice will be dictated by the tree, or trees, there already. Trees should be planted for harmony, not contrast. Those harmonise best which have a similar leaf shape.

If your trees are to be deciduous, then your hedges should be evergreen; if evergreen, then use either the brighter-leaved evergreens – Choisya, Griselinia, Euonymus japonica – or deciduous shrubs, perhaps those with autumn colour, as your hedges.

Do not mix large shiny leaves with woolly greyish ones, as for instance Aucubas and Magnolia grandiflora with Sorbus aria and

Figure 24 (*top left*)
Plan of a Three Tree Garden, using circles. The larger circle has had a path cut through it, with the tree planted in the inner circle, the shrubs in the outer one. From top to bottom: a Mountain, or a Manna, Ash; a False Acacia with two Rhus typhina Laciniata; a Chinese Angelica Tree.

Figure 25 (*top right*)
Plan of a Three Tree Garden, with a more eccentric solution. The trees are, top left, a Whitebeam; top right, a large-leaved Magnolia; bottom left, a Handkerchief Tree, or half-standard Fruit Tree, depending on its distance from the house. The shrubs are a mixture of Roses and Elder. With the trees placed thus, a circle or a square a little to the left of centre would also contain the shrubs extremely well.

Viburnum lantana. Do not associate a variegated tree with a variegated shrub; this would be altogether too restless. Do not mix silver and gold variegations; stick to one or the other. And do not attempt a garden composed *entirely* of large-leaved plants. The noise during a rain or wind storm would surprise you.

One tree that could be grown in a really large Three Tree Garden, and which has not been previously mentioned, is the Chinese Tree of Heaven, Ailanthus altissima. It is of extremely easy cultivation, growing all over London, for instance, in the most unlikely places. It will make a tree 30 feet, or 9 metres, through, and will grow much taller than that. So you must have space. It would associate particularly well with two other Chinese trees, Phellodendron amurense and Euodia hupehensis previously mentioned. The Ailanthus has very large pinnate leaves and strange bunches of tiny yellow flowers. It grows extremely fast and has an interesting bark. It has one drawback, a tendency to send out suckers, sometimes a long way from itself. It is so handsome that your neighbours may not mind but, in your own garden, you should cut them off.

On pages 122 and 123 there is a table with some suggestions for your Three Trees and their shrubs; and at figures 22-25 are some plans which may help you to lay out your Three Tree Garden.

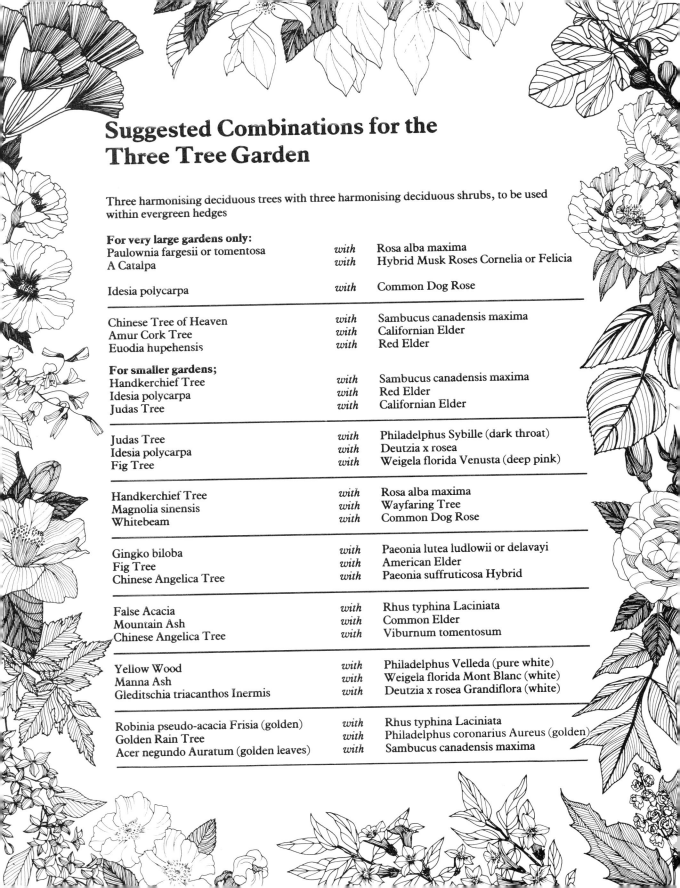

Suggested Combinations for the Three Tree Garden

Three harmonising deciduous trees with three harmonising deciduous shrubs, to be used within evergreen hedges

For very large gardens only:

Paulownia fargesii or tomentosa	*with*	Rosa alba maxima
A Catalpa	*with*	Hybrid Musk Roses Cornelia or Felicia
Idesia polycarpa	*with*	Common Dog Rose

Chinese Tree of Heaven	*with*	Sambucus canadensis maxima
Amur Cork Tree	*with*	Californian Elder
Euodia hupehensis	*with*	Red Elder

For smaller gardens;

Handkerchief Tree	*with*	Sambucus canadensis maxima
Idesia polycarpa	*with*	Red Elder
Judas Tree	*with*	Californian Elder

Judas Tree	*with*	Philadelphus Sybille (dark throat)
Idesia polycarpa	*with*	Deutzia x rosea
Fig Tree	*with*	Weigela florida Venusta (deep pink)

Handkerchief Tree	*with*	Rosa alba maxima
Magnolia sinensis	*with*	Wayfaring Tree
Whitebeam	*with*	Common Dog Rose

Gingko biloba	*with*	Paeonia lutea ludlowii or delavayi
Fig Tree	*with*	American Elder
Chinese Angelica Tree	*with*	Paeonia suffruticosa Hybrid

False Acacia	*with*	Rhus typhina Laciniata
Mountain Ash	*with*	Common Elder
Chinese Angelica Tree	*with*	Viburnum tomentosum

Yellow Wood	*with*	Philadelphus Velleda (pure white)
Manna Ash	*with*	Weigela florida Mont Blanc (white)
Gleditschia triacanthos Inermis	*with*	Deutzia x rosea Grandiflora (white)

Robinia pseudo-acacia Frisia (golden)	*with*	Rhus typhina Laciniata
Golden Rain Tree	*with*	Philadelphus coronarius Aureus (golden)
Acer negundo Auratum (golden leaves)	*with*	Sambucus canadensis maxima

Gleditschia triacanthos Inermis	*with*	Cornus alba Variegata (silver)
Acer negundo Variegatum (silver)	*with*	Californian Elder
Golden Rain Tree	*with*	Cornus alternifolia Argentea (silver)

Chinese Yellow Wood	*with*	Weigela florida Venusta (deep pink)
Manna Ash	*with*	Syringa persica Alba
Sorbaria arborea	*with*	Buddleia davidii Black Night

Euodia hupehensis	*with*	Philadelphus Velleda
Manna Ash	*with*	Deutzia x rosea Grandiflora
Service Tree (see page 141)	*with*	Weigela florida Mont Blanc

Amur Cork Tree	*with*	Philadelphus coronarius
Mountain Ash	*with*	Syringa persica Alba
Sorbaria arborea	*with*	Viburnum tomentosum

Whitebeam	*with*	Common Dogwood
Mountain Ash	*with*	Spindle Tree
Cockspur Thorn	*with*	Guelder Rose

Common Quince	*with*	Guelder Rose
Snowdrop Tree (the smaller Halesia carolina would be better if soil permits)	*with*	Hybrid Musk Rose Prosperity
Bird Cherry	*with*	Wayfaring Tree

3 Standard Apples	*with*	Guelder Rose
		Rosa rugosa alba
		Red Elder

3 Standard Pears	*with*	Hibiscus syriacus Elegantissimum
		Buddleia davidii White Bouquet
		Hybrid Musk Rose Prosperity

3 Standard Cherries	*with*	Syringa microphylla
		Weigela florida Conquete (pink)
		Buddleia davidii Charming (lavender)

3 Standard Plums	*with*	Common Dog Rose
		Guelder Rose
		Red Elder

FOUR TREES OR MORE

If you have four trees or more in your garden – or the space for them – you will probably be living in a handsome suburb, a village or on the edge of a country town. In either case, the fruit trees and decorative trees previously mentioned will still be in context; but the closer you are to the genuine country, the less sophisticated should be your hedges.

To the list of trees I would only add the Indian Chestnut (Aesculus indica) and the Sweet Buckeye (Aesculus flava or octandra), two rather smaller relations of the Horse Chestnut flowering a bit later, in early or midsummer. The Indian Chestnut has a greyish green leaf and a pink tinge to its flowers. It would look well with Whitebeam, Wayfaring Tree and the Jacobite Rose. The Sweet Buckeye has pale yellow, or deep cream, flowers and a very green leaf. It would look well with the Manna Ash, the Guelder Rose and yellow Hybrid Musks.

To them I would like to add the so-called Chinese Pagoda Tree, Sophora japonica, a tree not unlike the False Acacia but ultimately much larger and taking longer to flower. It is beautiful even as a young tree, however, but not, again, in cold or windy places. For association purposes it should be considered as a False Acacia.

If you have a garden of this size, and are hoping to convert it into a One Hour Garden, you are going to have to be rather firm, both with yourself and your nearest and dearest. Half measures will not prosper. The principal aim of your conversion is, quite simply, to bring the whole garden 'under the mower'.

You will need some tools in addition to your mower, which is probably better to be one of those that you sit on, with three or four different cutting levels. You will need a wheelbarrow, probably two; a stiff broom and a slightly stiffer one; a spade and a fork, as your neighbours are probably too distant, both in situation and manner, to be borrowed from; some long-handled pruners or a pair of lopping shears, but perhaps not both; a pruning saw, which is slightly curved; a rubber or wooden rake; and the shears, secateurs and long-handled handfork that we have had ever since the Minimum Garden.

Opposite
Magnolia mollicomata is one of the most splendid of the deciduous Magnolias, but it is only to be grown in neutral or acid soils.

Opposite
Magnolia sinensis will grow on a chalk, or limestone, soil, as long as it is both rich and deep.

First, you abolish all the paths, grassing them over. You do not need paths. Gumboots are cheap and easier to maintain. If you would like a flower border, then give yourself one quite large one, near the house and, if only accessible from one side, not more than three feet (90 cm.) wide. This is as far as a One Hour Gardener can reach without hurting his back. Any sheds should be brought into the House Complex, attached to the garage, or done away with altogether. The One Hour Gardener has very few tools and they can be stowed away in the garage which the Four Tree Gardener probably has.

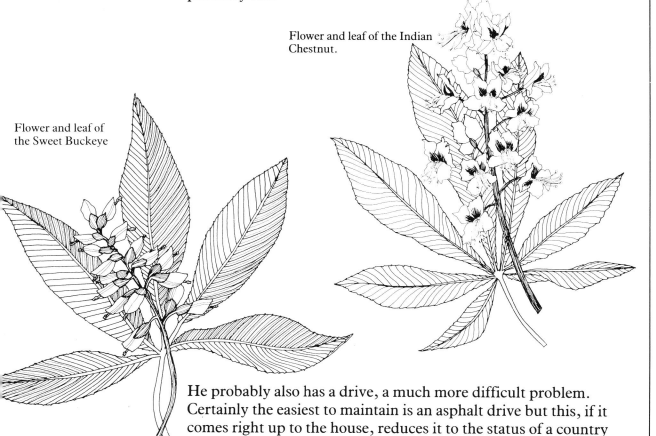

Flower and leaf of the Indian Chestnut.

Flower and leaf of the Sweet Buckeye

He probably also has a drive, a much more difficult problem. Certainly the easiest to maintain is an asphalt drive but this, if it comes right up to the house, reduces it to the status of a country pub or a country club, depending on its size. It should be separated from the house itself by a strip of paving (as in figure 29) or grass. If it has to be planted, use an amiable, low-growing shrub like Skimmia japonica and put it all the way along.

Gravel is the most agreeable material visually, but in general is rather a nuisance. It must be treated with weed-killer in the spring – you may need a watering can for that – needs raking and must, especially, be entirely cleared of leaves in the autumn, otherwise it will go all mossy and disgusting.

If you are having to make your drive, then have two ribbons, or tyre tracks, set slightly below the level of the grass so that the mower can glide over them. The ribbons can be made of brick, or stone, or concrete slabs or, of course, asphalt. This is the easiest kind of drive to maintain that is also pleasant to look at.

Overgrown shrubberies and shrub borders are going to require strength, both of arm and mind. It is sometimes possible to reduce one to a mixed, or 'tapestry', hedge. I would never advocate planting one, but if this is the simple solution to that sad phalanx of miserable plants, which even the birds have ceased to visit, by all means adopt it.

The alternative is to thin it out, leaving only the plants that you really like yourself, far enough away from each other to make their own natural shape. Six feet (1.80 m.) is the absolute minimum for this and would also let the mower through. With luck, you may find that some of the shrubs released will make small trees.

Having decided where you want – if you want – your one big flower border, put all the herbaceous plants in it and grass over the existing flower beds, which are probably all over the place. There has been a fashion in recent years for raised borders, possibly designed to make weeding easier but always requiring a great deal of water. These too should be removed and covered with grass. The one question to ask yourself is: 'Can I get the mower over, through or round it?'

If that is all you need to do well and good. What is far more likely, unfortunately, is that you have inadvertently acquired, or perhaps have inherited, a mid-twentieth century Horror Garden and are wondering what on earth to do with it.

A Garden of Golden Leaves

Already mentioned:

Trees	Shrubs
Robinia pseudo-acacia Frisia	Golden Elder, Sambucus nigra Aurea
Gleditschia triacanthos Sunburst	Sambucus canadensis Aurea
Acer negundo Auratum	Sambucus racemosa Plumosa Aurea
Catalpa bignonoides Aurea	Philadelphus coronarius Aureus
Laburnum anagyroides Aureum	Golden Privet, Ligustrum ovalifolium
	aureo-marginatum

Also:

Acer pseudo-platanus Corstorphinense (the Corstorphine Plane) and Acer pseudo-platanus Worlei (the Golden Sycamore) are two kinds of Sycamore whose young leaves are a soft yellow, passing to a deeper yellow in midsummer, finally turning green. They make large trees and should not be attempted in a small garden.

Weigela florida Looymansii Aurea is a yellow-leaved Weigela with pink flowers. Its drawback is that its leaves burn in the sun and it is therefore only to be successfully planted in the shade, either of its attendant tree or of a sheltering hedge.

Ribes sanguineum Brocklebankii is a golden-leaved flowering currant also with pink flowers, and with exactly the same problem as the yellow-leaved Weigela. Both will grow facing the north, though not in exposed positions, but they may not flower, no particular hardship in either case.

Hedges

A Garden of Golden Leaves is best surrounded by evergreen hedges of a very dark green, that is to say of Yew, Holm Oak, Holly, Escallonia, Laurustinus, Osmanthus, Phillyrea, Osmarea, Lonicera nitida or Elaeagnus ebingii. The Golden Privet makes an excellent hedge, but it is extremely vigorous and may require clipping as many as four times in a damp summer. The Golden Beech (Fagus sylvatica Zlatia) would make a most beautiful hedge but might be rather expensive to plant. It would do well as a transverse hedge, as would any of the Elders mentioned above, grown free. Obviously, the Golden Beech could also be grown as a tree, but it does get very large in the end.

A garden in which trees, shrubs and hedges *all* had golden leaves might be a bit too much.

THE HORROR GARDEN DISPLAYED

The mid-twentieth century Horror Garden accurately reflects the society which produced it, being shapeless, formless, aimless, divided into agitated little groups not related, and not speaking, to each other and being about as labour-intensive as is possible, as though there were a fear of redundancy even here.

It also demonstrates quite incidentally the national passion for concentrating on irrelevant side issues. Individually, each 'vignette' may be charming, perfectly worthy of a glossy magazine's photographer. But nothing adds up. The garden turns in upon itself, a confusion of nervous details, reflecting principally the under-lying anxieties of its owner.

Often, there is a very strong fantasy factor, a desire to create a false environment with little or no relation to anything around it, as far as possible from Alexander Pope's precept: 'Consult the genius of the place in all.' The 'place' no longer has a 'genius'; its own

Key to PLAN OF HORROR GARDEN

1.	Garden Shed	17.	Island bed for Herbaceous Planting
2.	Hedge of Leyland Cypress	18.	Stepping Stones in Grass, leading to
3.	Birch Grove	19.	Asphalt Path
4.	Random Shrubs	20.	Crazy Paving Path
5.	Chestnut Tree	21.	Ash Tree
6.	Christmas Tree 1978	22.	Group of Weeping Willows
7.	Thicket of Lilac and Laburnum	23.	Group of Flowering Cherries
8.	Avenue of Siberian Crab Apples	24.	Bed of Floribunda Roses
9.	Sycamore Tree	25.	House
10.	Real Fruit Trees	26.	Garage
11.	Wavy Line Flower Border	27.	Heather Garden
12.	Christmas Tree 1972	28.	Impenetrable Shrubbery
13.	Wendy House	29.	Christmas Tree 1968
14.	Tree with non-green leaves	30.	Crazy Paving Path to Front Door
15.	Groups of Dwarf Conifers	31.	Surprisingly Nice Tree
16.	Pool with Rockery and Alpine Planting	32.	Asphalt Drive

Figure 26
The Horror Garden Displayed.

character is entirely concealed by little ponds and little paths, little bumps and little marshes, tiny terraces, mini-mountains, mostly covered with plants which could not possibly exist there naturally and which, indeed, would die without the frequent attention of their owner. In short, it is a private, sheltered place in which to play at being God.

They could be called Ostrich Gardens, or Magpie Gardens, since many of the plants in them are only there because the owner saw a picture in a magazine, or read about it in a newspaper – not because it looks well with what is already there, not because the soil is precisely right for it, not even because the owner likes it. Merely, he didn't have one before.

At figure 26 you will find a plan of such a garden, based on a real one near Worthing. Here you will find a tiny lake backed by a tiny mountain with a tiny alpine meadow in front of it (16), so that the owner may imagine himself in Switzerland. Here is a Birch Grove (3) and a Heather Garden (27), so that he may imagine himself in Scotland, a Wendy House which takes him to the Never Never Land (13), an asphalt path (19) lined by Siberian Crab Apples (8) leading to a remote hut (1) screened by sinister Leyland Cypresses (2) so that he may imagine himself in a Russian Labour Camp.

Trees from three particularly memorable Christmases (6, 12 and 29) loom here and there, the Norwegian Spruce being one of the tallest trees that grows in Britain. Free-form beds of flowers (17) and floribunda roses (24) trip one up at every turn. A free-form Swimming Pool was planned above the Heather Garden, a tennis court in the top right-hand corner. There are Dwarf Conifers (15), stepping stones across the lawn (18), a Wavy Line Border down the whole of one side (11), two impenetrable shrubberies. . . .

To keep such a garden, of rather more than an acre (.4 hectares), in even bad order, would require three or four hours a day in spring, summer and autumn, and constant attention in the winter, perhaps half-an-hour a day.

Probably it is not possible to convert such a garden into a One Hour Garden, but we can try. Perhaps a One and a Half Hour Garden.

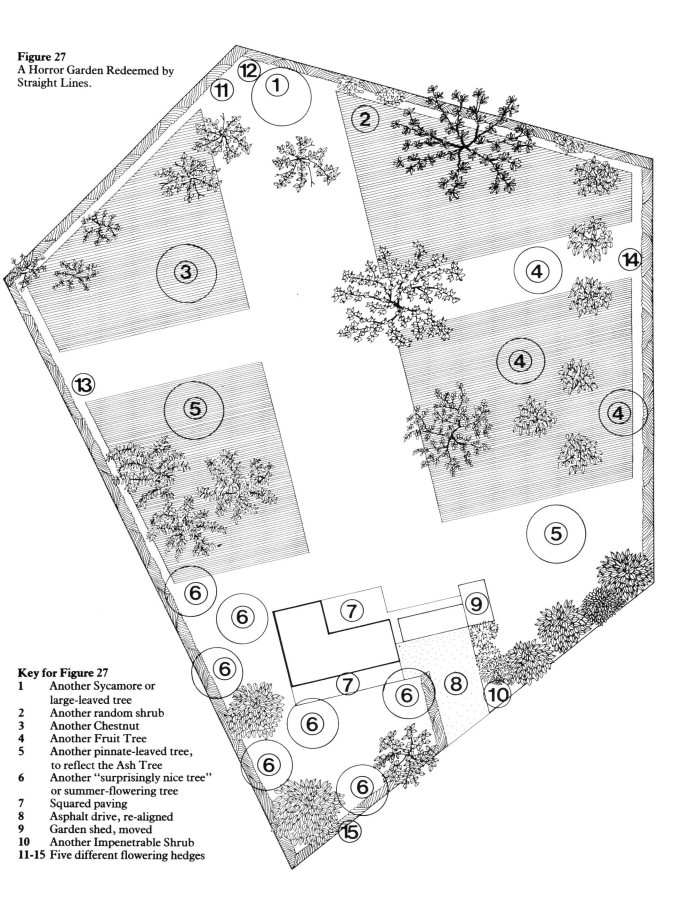

Figure 27
A Horror Garden Redeemed by
Straight Lines.

Key for Figure 27
1   Another Sycamore or
    large-leaved tree
2   Another random shrub
3   Another Chestnut
4   Another Fruit Tree
5   Another pinnate-leaved tree,
    to reflect the Ash Tree
6   Another "surprisingly nice tree"
    or summer-flowering tree
7   Squared paving
8   Asphalt drive, re-aligned
9   Garden shed, moved
10 Another Impenetrable Shrub
11-15 Five different flowering hedges

THE HORROR GARDEN REDEEMED

A conversion of this kind is as much a test of character as it is of physical strength. One must cease to pretend, to wish oneself otherwise, and must accept the limits and limitations of one's own ground even if, as in this case, the outside shape is very unhelpful.

A garden in England is, presumably, an English Garden which should reflect its countryside. The English countryside, as we have inherited it, consists of hedges, trees and fields, of grass and grain and low growing crops, giving a continuous surface over a wide area. In Scotland and Wales there are contours to contend with and the simple remedies suggested previously in this book may appear a little too simple; but the principles stand.

The ancestor of this kind of garden is the early eighteenth century English Garden, like the one at Studley Royal in Yorkshire. It consists of formalised water, some formalised contours, natural woodland contained by a Yew hedge and, in the principal perspective, only one building, a Greek temple. It is enormous, but the maintenance is minimal, the grass to cut, the Yew to clip once a year. It is interesting even in midwinter because it has such excellent 'bones'. Most of the gardens like this were destroyed in the days of 'Capability' Brown.

Something like this must be our aim – though I do not advocate water in a One Hour Garden – but there is a word of warning. If you live in a Conservation Area you will be subject to a Committee. Most Conservation Committees are under the immovable impression that precisely the correct number of trees has already been planted. If you cut one down, you must plant another, whether there is room for it or not. If, therefore, your garden is already hopelessly overplanted, it is probably better to do nothing. Conservationists, in their way, are quite as ruthless as Destructionists.

For our purposes, the gardens achieved at figures 27, 28 and 29 are not in Conservation Areas. The numbers in the text continue to refer to figure 26.

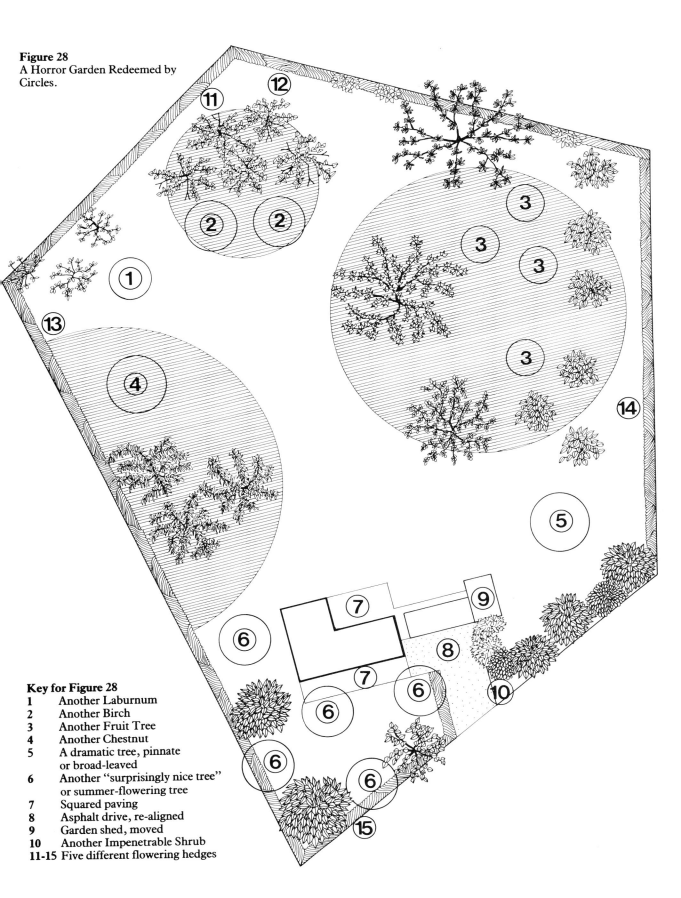

Figure 28
A Horror Garden Redeemed by
Circles.

Key for Figure 28
1   Another Laburnum
2   Another Birch
3   Another Fruit Tree
4   Another Chestnut
5   A dramatic tree, pinnate
    or broad-leaved
6   Another "surprisingly nice tree"
    or summer-flowering tree
7   Squared paving
8   Asphalt drive, re-aligned
9   Garden shed, moved
10 Another Impenetrable Shrub
11-15 Five different flowering hedges

To begin with, all the Cosmetic Features have been removed, that is to say the Alpine Section and all the Flower Beds and Paths. The Rockery was, in this case, false; of course if you have a natural outcrop of rock in your garden you make it a centre of attention. The Garden Shed (1) has been brought down and attached to the Garage (26). The Flower Border, if there is going to be one, should be near the house and a good place, assuming it does not face due north, would be alongside the extension to the new terrace now leading to the new Garden Shed.

The Laburnum (3) and Birch Groves (7) remain, judiciously thinned. With the Asphalt Path (19) removed the Siberian Crabs (8) no longer have a function, neither do they make an agreeable group without it. The Japanese Cherries (23) have been cut down but only because they occupy space that could be used by something more interesting. Placed as they are, they could remain. The Impenetrable Shrubberies (28) have been thinned, as suggested on page 125.

In the Worthing garden there was one 'surprisingly nice tree' (31), in this case a young and beautiful Silver Lime. If you are planting new trees you should take into account what is already there.

The Christmas Trees have been removed, and the hedge of Leyland Cypress down one side. The Leyland Cypress can grow well over ninety feet (27 m.) and will do so with amazing speed. After ten years a hedge of it will become a nightmare to maintain. Remove it while you can.

I remain unrepentant on the subject of the containing hedges. They give an amiable character to any garden, if chosen properly, and offer a discernible framework. They do not all have to be planted at once; in this case the cost might be enormous. You can plant one side a year – in this case – for the next five years, beginning at the front. Neither do they all have to be clipped in one day. In England, the end of July and beginning of August is a good time to clip all the hedges I have suggested, but you can do so right into October, or until the first frost.

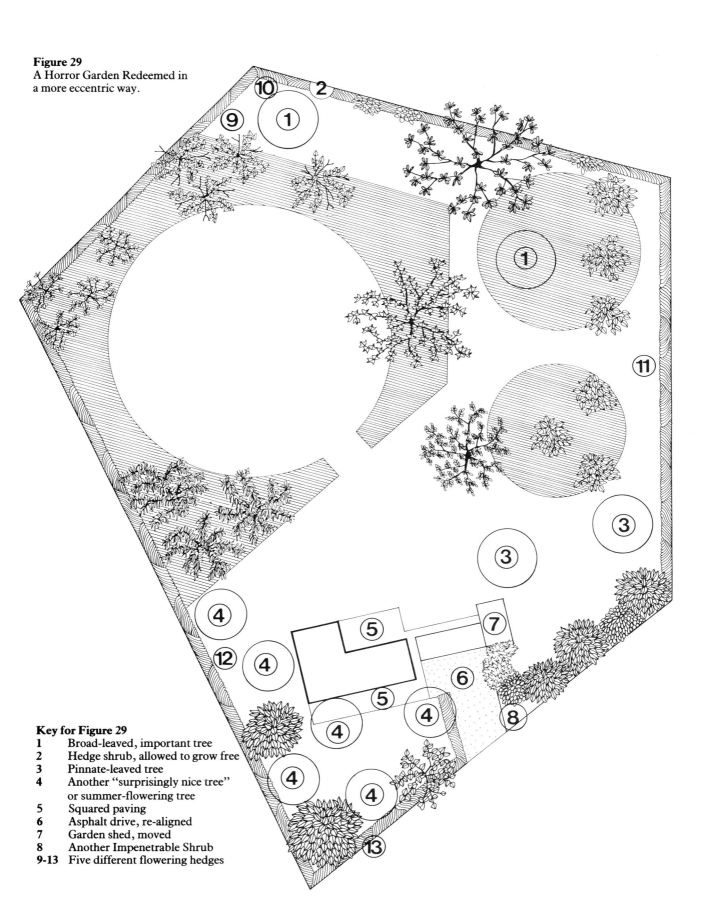

Figure 29
A Horror Garden Redeemed in a more eccentric way.

Key for Figure 29

1   Broad-leaved, important tree
2   Hedge shrub, allowed to grow free
3   Pinnate-leaved tree
4   Another "surprisingly nice tree"
    or summer-flowering tree
5   Squared paving
6   Asphalt drive, re-aligned
7   Garden shed, moved
8   Another Impenetrable Shrub
9-13 Five different flowering hedges

Except the Choisya and the Skimmia, the smaller Escallonias and the Roses – which are entirely unsuitable as boundary hedges – all the recommended hedges will achieve six or seven feet. In time.

You will need some help to do all this. If you are lucky, the Rockery will just fill the little pond. Bear in mind that grass must have at least six inches (15 cms.) of soil below it to grow well. The Crazy Paving could well be sold to, or taken away by, a Keen Gardener or a Garden Centre. The Stepping Stones might be included in the new terrace. The Asphalt Path – let us hope it is not actually made of concrete – may well have to be carved up with a pneumatic drill and used only as hardcore, and this applies also to the re-alignment of the front drive. You may also need some new topsoil to fill in the depressions left by departed paths.

The garden at figure 26 is perfectly flat. Quite possibly you have some little bumps, so beloved of garden designers in the 'Sixties, or even some natural contours. The former can probably be flattened and may even turn out to be made of perfectly good topsoil. If one of them is concealing an old air raid shelter, it might well be worth paying to get rid of it. It will be of no use in the next war.

If your contours are natural, then they will give you the shapes for your garden. Keep the 'hills' as longer grass, the 'valleys' as lawn.

It may take time, it may take money, but I submit that it will be worth it in the end. You will have a garden with which you can be friends. A burden will have dropped from your shoulders.

FOUR TREES OR MORE & COUNTRY GARDENS

The One Hour Country Garden differs from the One Hour Town and Suburban Garden only in the kind of plants used. If you live in the true country, with fields nearby and a Genuine Rural View available from some portion of your house, you will be wiser to plant either the native shrubs and trees, or something very closely resembling them.

If you should need formal hedging, then Holly, Lime, Hornbeam, Beech, Hedge Maple, Guelder Rose and the Common Dogwood are the most suitable. But if you think of planting a Hedgerow – that is to say an informal mixed hedge cut only every three or four years – then Holly, Hedge Maple, Guelder Rose, Wayfaring Tree, Spindle Tree, Dogwood, Elder, the native Privet, Hawthorn, Blackthorn and Hazel make an excellent mixture. The Hazel and the Holly should be allowed to make trees, perhaps the Hedge Maple as well. They should be spaced at three feet (90 cm.) and very well mixed.

Any of these last – except perhaps the Hawthorn and the Blackthorn – can be grown in the garden as shrubs. Of the more 'gardeny' shrubs previously mentioned, the Lilacs and the

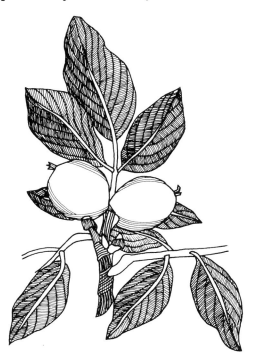

Leaf and fruit of the Walnut.

Philadelphuses, especially the large ones, look well with the native shrubs. The Weigelas also look at home in the country, Hydrangea paniculata Grandiflora when grown in grass, and all the Shrub Roses.

This has become a very large term, but I take it to mean the Gallicas, the Albas, the Damasks, the Centifolias, the Moss Roses, the Bourbons, the Hybrid Perpetuals, the Hybrid Musks, certain recent Spinossissima hybrids – from the native Burnet Rose – and all the rose species, much neglected. They will all grow well in the grass though, as usual, you must take care it does not strangle them.

Leaf and fruit of the Oriental Plane

If you are planting trees in a country garden, I could never conscientiously recommend anything other than fruit trees unless a very large tree were required. If, for instance, you have a lawn tennis court somewhere, and your tennis days are over, it could look quite sensible planted formally as an orchard.

As a specimen tree the Service Tree (Sorbus domestica) looks very well in such surroundings; it is a native tree incredibly difficult to obtain. The other natives previously mentioned – the Whitebeam, Rowan and Bird Cherry – are also suitable for such a planting. If you feel you have to plant a Flowering Cherry, why not plant a Fruiting Cherry instead?

The Quince, the Mulberry and the Medlar, all previously mentioned, are all very much at home in a country garden.

The False Acacia is happy near a house, and the native Aspen (Populus tremula) is an extremely beautiful tree hardly ever planted. Both of these look best in groups of three, or five, or seven, and they blend together very well.

If you *have* to plant an evergreen tree then it should be a Yew or a Holm Oak (Quercus ilex), depending on the size required. The Oak is, in particular, a gesture towards the future as it transplants only very young, and therefore very small. It is a charming plant at all stages, however.

The Walnut (Juglans nigra or regia), and the Horse Chestnut (Aesculus hippocastanum), are both particularly handsome trees, but look better in conjunction with some sort of building, the house, or a barn or cowshed. That is to say they tend, in my opinion, to look a little uncomfortable growing alone in a field surrounded by British Natives – Oak, Ash, Beech, Hornbeam, Birch, Poplar, Willow, Lime and Alder.

The same applies to the Oriental Plane (Platanus orientalis), and the Tulip Tree (Liriodendron tulipifera), two of the most magnificent trees which grow in England; but they look superb viewed at the same time as some handsome building.

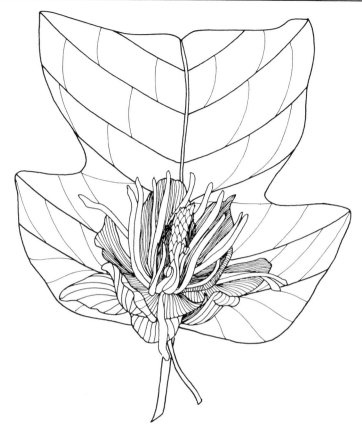

Flower and leaf of the Tulip Tree.

All these make very large trees in the end, with a head of between thirty and fifty feet (9 and 15 metres) in a hundred years. They are all suitable for making avenues in the full country and would make very splendid ones. Of the native trees, now that we no longer have any Elms, Oak, Beech, Hornbeam and Lime are the best for this purpose. As an 'Elm substitute' I would like to recommend Zelkova carpinifolia, a Caucasian tree with echoes of both the Hornbeam and the Elm.

Finally, the Sycamore (Acer pseudo-platanus), though not native, has been here so long that it looks comfortable anywhere there is room for it. It is also a good avenue tree. It has a number of coloured-leaved varieties, including some very beautiful cream and pale yellow variegations, but I am not sure that these look well in the open countryside, any more than I really think that the Copper Beech looks well against a green background.

The green Sycamore is unbelievably prolific so, if you are including it in your garden, make sure it is growing in grass so that the mower can murder the seedlings. It is particularly fond of neglected gravel paths and decaying paving, but of course you no longer have either of these in your One Hour Garden.

Opposite
The Portugal Laurel, Prunus lusitanica, makes a handsome hedge in relatively large gardens, or an elegant evergreen tree.

Overleaf
The Cherry Laurel, Prunus laurocerasus, is only suitable for hedging on a really enormous scale, but it makes a dramatic, rather tropical-looking, evergreen tree.

A Garden of British Natives

Already mentioned:

Trees
The Whitebeam, Sorbus aria
The Mountain Ash, Sorbus aucuparia
The Bird Cherry, Prunus padus
The Hedge Maple, Acer campestre

Shrubs
The Wayfaring Tree, Viburnum lantana
The Guelder Rose, Viburnum opulus
The Common Elder, Sambucus nigra
The Dog Rose, Rosa canina
The Common Dogwood, Cornus sanguinea
The Common Privet, Ligustrum vulgare

Hedges
Yew – Holly – Box – Guelder Rose – Hedge Maple – Common Dogwood – Common Privet

Also:
Malus pumila is one of the native Crab Apples, perhaps the easiest to obtain. The other is called Malus sylvestris.

The Sand Pear, Pyrus pyrifolia, is about as close as one can come to the native Pear, Pyrus communis, now almost unobtainable.

The Gean, Prunus avium, and its variety, plena, are the native Cherries but their fruit is really only suitable for the birds. Plena can make a particularly large tree.

The Myrobalan Plum (Prunus cerasifera) is only doubtfully native but only purists will object to its inclusion here.

The Service Tree, Sorbus domestica, is an extremely beautiful tree now almost impossible to find. Its fruit, called Serves, was much eaten at the end of the sixteenth century.

The native Hawthorns, Crataegus monogyna and Crataegus oxycantha, make very tough small trees. Both are very slow-growing and for this reason have not been recommended otherwise. They look superb both in flower and fruit, their 'haws' passing from a deep scarlet to crimson. Both will make prickly hedges that do not flower, as they must be clipped tight, as will the Common Blackthorn, or Sloe. They are suitable as hedging plants only in the full country.

Clearly, such a garden would give you less trouble than anything else, but it must be said that, unless you have room for the evergreen hedges – Yew, Holly, Box and Common Privet – it will not look very interesting in the winter.

CONCRETE GARDENS & FRONT AND BACK YARDS

To cover your front or back garden with a plain layer of cement is to admit that you are no longer interested in life, that the circumstances of your existence have taken over and vanquished you.

The alternatives are not very many, but you can cover the area with something other than cement and leave a space for growing something *in the ground*. Tubs and pots all need more attention than you are prepared to give, but a mature plant with its roots actually in the soil will need watering only in times of official drought.

For present purposes I am assuming that your Front or Back Yard is smaller than the Absolute Minimum Garden (page 6), that is to say that the other side of it is less than fifteen feet (4.50 m.) from the house. I am also assuming that it is in an industrial town or city. The plants suggested are presented with the hardiest first, that is to say the Fatsia is the toughest, the Phormium the tenderest. You will have to make up your own mind about the shrubs for the Two Foot Square (page 147).

Natural stone is the handsomest paving and the most expensive. Brick is charming, unless it is very badly laid, and a particularly good background to the kind of evergreens you will be growing. Concrete paving always looks like exactly what it is, a cheap substitute for stone, but there are now several kinds of paving stone made of natural stone and cement dust and some of these are very handsome. There are also some natural-coloured, artificially-grained paving stones which look very well properly laid. Some of them come in a length that is twice its width so that they can be laid 'basket pattern' – two together and then two together at right angles to them.

Granite setts and sea-washed pebbles should be avoided as everyone throws their cigarette ends into them. Bands of brick let into paving will look all right if the bands are wide enough, at least the width of two bricks. Bricks can be laid 'basket pattern' in twos, on their backs, or in threes, on their sides, the second being the more satisfactory. If you have to Crazy Pave it then use only Crazy Paving from side to side – it looks much better on its own.

In your paving, leave a planting area 2 foot, 4 foot or 6 foot square (60 cm., 1.20 or 1.80 m.), depending on your enthusiasm, or a long bed 3 foot by 9 (90 cm. by 2.70 m.), depending on the shape of your yard. Dig this area well, to a depth of at least 2 feet (60 cm.), and dig in a generous amount of manure or vegetable compost. This will give you much better plants and save you trouble in the end.

The Two Foot Square

This requires one shrub only. If you are having only one square, make it well to one side of your yard – that is to say do not place it centrally. If you are having two squares, then place them symmetrically; if three, then the third can be in the middle.

For the first year or two, before the shrub has filled the space, you may have to do a little weeding. You could plant any of the following evergreen shrubs, all described elsewhere in this book. If you are having two squares, you should plant two of the same shrub; if three, two of one kind and one of another, the 'one' in the middle.

South and West facing:
Choisya ternata
Griselinia littoralis
Any Escallonia
Osmanthus delavayi or
   ilicifolia
Phillyrea decora
Camellia japonica

North and East facing:
Viburnum tinus
Skimmia japonica
Euonymous japonica and
   varieties
Any Pyracantha (which you
   may have to clip)
Aucuba japonica

If you do not live in a clean air area, or if you suffer from any kind of industrial pollution, then plant either Euonymus or Aucuba. They are the toughest.

Any of these shrubs can be used in place of the Fatsia, the Privet, the Yucca or the Phormium in the following planting suggestions.

The Four Foot Square

This should be at one side of your yard,
not in the middle, about
two feet (60 cm.) from the back and side walls.

If it is in the top right hand corner then plant, in the top right hand corner of your square, a Fatsia japonica. In the top left hand corner, plant a Fatshedera lizei, in the bottom left corner a Hedera hibernica (the Irish Ivy) and in the bottom right hand corner another Fatshedera. The Fatshedera is a hybrid between the Fatsia and the Hedera and they all look very well together. They will fill your yard quite quickly – I am assuming that you need no space in it for yourself – but you can nip their growing tips in the spring, if they offer to come in at the window.

In place of the Fatsia, you could plant a Chinese Privet (Ligustrum lucidum), if it has room to grow to fifteen feet without shading one of your windows. It has variegated varieties which would be in context here. With it plant two Fatshedera as before – there is one with a cream variegation – and one Ivy as before. The best variegated Ivy is called Hedera canariensis Variegata. Probably it is better not to have everything variegated. With a plain tree variegated creepers and plain creepers with a variegated tree.

Or you could plant three Yucca, top left, bottom left and bottom right. In the top right hand corner plant one variegated Ivy, or Fatshedera, and let it creep through.

Or you can plant one Phormium tenax in the top right hand corner, but only if your yard is sheltered and gets some sun. With it a variegated Ivy or Fatshedera will look best. Neither the Yucca nor the Phormium will tolerate anything other than Clean Air. The Phormium is a magnificent foliage plant with sword-like leaves of a dark green which can grow up to, and more than, six feet (1.80 m.).

If your square is in the left hand corner of your yard, then for 'right' read 'left' and *vice versa*.

A Four Foot Square: Fatsia japonica underplanted with Fatshedera and Irish Ivy.

The Six Foot Square

Rather more ambitious this. In one corner, as before, the Fatsia, the Privet, the Yucca – but only one this time – or the Phormium.

With the Fatsia, three Choisyas, three Skimmias or one Aucuba, underplanted with one Ivy or Fatshedera, plain or variegated, placed so that it will spread towards the light.

With the Privet, three Camellias, three Euonymus japonica, three medium sized Escallonias or one Aucuba, underplanted as above, on the same principle.

With the Yucca, three Skimmias, three Choisyas, or three Phillyrea decora, underplanted as above.

With the Phormium, three Skimmias or three Phillyrea decora, with the underplanting as before.

One of the group of three should be planted in the corner opposite to the 'tree', with the other two over its left and right shoulders. There should be a space between the group and the 'tree', to be filled by the underplant.

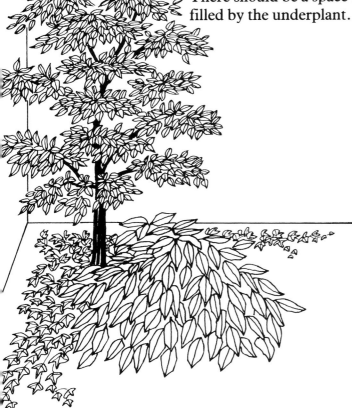

A Six Foot Square: Ligustrum lucidum, with an Aucuba in front, underplanted with Ivy.

The Three by Nine

At one end, the Fatsia, the Privet, three Yucca (in a V) or the Phormium. At the other end, in an inverted V, three of any of the shrubs suggested for the Two Foot Square – you would certainly have to keep the Pyracantha down if you choose it. One underplant placed centrally, and encouraged to grow in both directions, should be enough.

I have assumed that your yard does not face due north into a high wall, and that it is not totally in the shadow of your house. All the plants suggested must have some sun – the more they have the more they are likely to flower. Therefore place your planting area where the sun stays longest.

If your yard does face north and gets no sun, just pave it over entirely and purchase an object, bearing in mind that nothing looks more dreadful than a naked marble female trying to retain her draperies in a high wind in February. Your object should be of stone, or wood – even painted metal looks chillsome in the winter.

A Three by Nine: Phormium tenax (L) and three Camellias underplanted with Ivy.

SIMPLE FLOWER BORDERS

Much against my better judgment, I offer these few simple suggestions. Flowers have really no place in a One Hour Garden, but the owner of such a garden is going to find himself subjected to such shrieks from his sisters-in-law – 'No *colour*' – 'Always the *same*' – 'So *dull*' – that I include them in the humblest spirit of Christian goodwill.

Flower borders should consist of herbaceous plants only, that is to say plants grown primarily for their flowers and which die down, and disappear, during the winter. Herbaceous borders always look awful in the winter. Initially, they should be deeply dug, to a depth of at least two feet (60 cm.), and generously manured before planting. After that they can be 'top-dressed' either with manure, or compost, or lime, or all three depending on your soil, every year, or every other year, or never again, depending entirely on you, and this is best done – in my opinion: ask any four gardeners the same question and you will get four different answers, all probably perfectly correct – in November in England, that is to say at the end of the autumn.

You may have to add a trowel to the stock of tools already mentioned. You should weed your border very carefully in the middle of spring, as soon as it is warm enough to make this other than a penance. With luck, and if you are thorough enough, you may not have to do it again until the autumn, when you are cutting the plants down for the winter.

Close planting is the secret here. Herbaceous plants like to grow together, to touch one another. Nothing is more intimidating to them than to find themselves standing alone in a desolate plain of neatly raked soil, unable to contact their friends.

Your border is best attached visually to your house. That is to say, it should be on one side of the terrace on which you sit; or it should run along the south front of your house; or it should be on one side of your front path. Alternatively, it could well take the place of a Transverse Hedge in the Minimum Garden.

Ideally it should run east and west. If it does have to run north and south, make sure that the sun is on it for at least half the day. It should be no more than three feet wide (90 cm.) and preferably accessible from both sides, permitting the weeder to operate without too many gymnastics.

If it has grass on one side of it, or on both, it is worth putting a brick or stone edging down it at least nine inches (23½ cm.) wide – the length of a brick, for instance – so that the mower can do the edging and the flowers can grow right up to the edge of the border without being assaulted by the afore-mentioned mower every time the grass is cut.

In April and May, from mid to late spring, unless you have interplanted your herbaceous plants with tulips (which is rather a good idea) your border will consist only of leaves. But there will be some flowers in the border from June till the end of October, early summer until the first frost.

I am a block planter myself, as is clear from the plan which I offer. Borders are easier to plant in this way, there are no awkward corners and the plants join up more quickly. The quantities suggested – as your Keen Gardening friends will certainly tell you – are in support of my statement that 'close planting is the secret' – of minimum weeding.

The border I am offering is three feet by eighteen, 90 centimetres by 5.40 metres. It can be lengthened by choosing a square that takes your fancy and adding it on at either end. I do not recommend shortening it. If you have to do this, you have really not enough room for this kind of border.

There are two colour ways, one with a stone, or concrete, house behind it – grey anyway – the other with a brick house behind it. If your house is colour washed, you must make up your own mind which to choose.

BORDER A (overleaf)

For a Grey Background

Pale yellows, cream, white, several pinks, very dark purple, dark blue

1. Herbaceous Peonies. Some of the most beautiful flowers that grow in this climate, originally native to China, Japan, Korea and

Mongolia, now extensively hybridised. I suggest Sarah Bernhardt, a luscious double pink, and the Duke of Wellington, an equally luscious double white, five of one and four of the other. The only things that will infallibly kill peonies are to expose their tubers to frost or to plant them so that they are standing in water the whole winter. They will probably not flower for the first two years, but will do so thereafter in increasing size and splendour just as spring turns into summer. They like plenty of manure.

2. Iris germanica Hybrids. I propose the magnificent Black Ink, a very dark purple indeed, interplanted alternately with the equally magnificent Cliffs of Dover, a superb white. Four of each. Plant them with their rhizomes – the fleshy stem part – facing, and exposed to, the sun. If your soil is neutral to acid, give them some lime in the spring. Mid to late summer.

3. Anemone japonica. A marvellous border plant, flowering from early autumn until the first frost, tall and elegant with especially handsome leaves. Not easy to establish, so be rather patient, but once they are established they will flower generously for a long time every year. White Queen is a very good white, Queen Charlotte a very good pink. Interplant them like the Irises, four of each.

4. Hemerocallis. The Day Lilies are so called because each individual flower lasts only one day, but they carry several buds on each head and their combined flowering period covers several weeks. Again, they are slow to start but more or less indestructible once established. I suggest a combination of Halo Light, a creamy pink, and Shooting Star, a creamy yellow. Eight, interplanted as before. Mid to late summer.

5. Salvia superba East Friesland. Dark purple blue spikes coming from a solid rosette of soft grey-green leaves, producing a solid mass of colour when in flower. It is a reliable plant, flowering early in its life, but it does demand uninterrupted sun. Eight. Mid to late summer.

6. Lupin Patricia of York. Hybridisers of the last fifty years have gone all out for the multi-coloured Lupin, most of which are objects of unadulterated horror impossible to include in any civilised colour scheme. This is a pure, pale yellow which will flower from early to late summer if you dead-head it regularly. Nine.

7. Monkshood, Aconitum napellus Bressingham Spire. A tall, very handsome dark blue-purple spike not unlike a Delphinium, but much stronger, hardier, and not in need of staking. Its roots are poisonous but only if eaten. It is trouble-free once established, but is slow to begin flowering, perhaps not until its third year. Late summer. Nine.

8. Verbascum Hybrids. Excellent garden relations of our native Mullein, they have spires of flowers not unlike those of the Hollyhock, but much smaller. Their leaves are particularly handsome and they much prefer a touch of lime in the soil. I suggest a mixture of Gainsborough, a pale yellow, and Mont Blanc, a good white, interplanted as before. Will flower the whole summer if you are lucky. Six, three of each.

9. Sidalcea Rose Queen. A delicate-looking spire of pink flowers not unlike those of the Common Mallow (if that means anything). An 'old-fashioned' flower of great style and charm, with a fine constitution. Mid to late summer, sometimes on into a good autumn. Eight.

BORDER B (previous page)

For a Brick Background
Yellows, white and cream

1. Herbaceous Peonies. The Duke of Wellington again, this time with the Duchesse de Nemours, a wonderful double cream. Four and five, late spring to early summer.

2. Iris germanica Hybrids. This time Desert Song, cream and white, and Gold Flake, deep yellow and cream. Interplant alternately, four of each. Mid to late summer.

3. Anemone japonica. Only white this time, White Queen, Louise Uhink and/or Honorine Joubert. Eight altogether. Early to mid autumn.

10. Centaurea macrocephala. A superb strong plant with soft, unprickly yellow flowers like a thistle. Your sisters-in-law will want to know what this is. Easy to grow, amazingly little known, a relation of our native Knapweed. Midsummer. Plant three in a V, or five in a W if you are in a hurry. It also takes time to flower.

11. Geum Lady Stratheden. A very handsome double yellow relation of one of our own wild flowers, the Meadow Avens. Comes from a rosette of deeply-cut leaves, flowering the whole summer if dead-headed. Eight.

6. Lupin Canary Bird. Another self-coloured Lupin of splendid appearance and constitution, slightly darker and brighter than Patricia of York, a beautiful yellow. Will flower all summer if dead-headed. Nine.

12. Chrysanthemum maximum H. Seibert. In no way resembling the Chrysanths of christenings, weddings, funerals, elections, birthdays, memorial services, concerts, etc., this superb plant has large white single daisy flowers with slightly frilled petals, flowering the entire summer and beyond if dead-headed. Nine.

8. Verbascum Hybrids, as before, Gainsborough and Mont Blanc. Three of each, flowering throughout the summer if you are lucky.

13. Anthemis tinctoria, either Mrs E.C. Buxton, a strong, clear yellow, or Wargrave Variety, rather paler. Or both. A tall, strong daisy with yellow centre and yellow petals, flowering the whole summer if dead-headed. Eight altogether.

Please do not think that I think that these are Borders to End All Borders. They are plants that will give you no trouble once they are established – like babies they require a bit of help in the first two years – but they will give something of colour and interest during the months of summer without demanding your constant attendance. And they will repay over and over again any care and attention that you choose to bestow on them, as indeed, I think I can say, will all the plants mentioned in this book.

Nothing is guaranteed in gardening, any more than it is in life. The plants I have suggested throughout this book are plants of distinction and interest, unusual, in some cases unknown (and quite probably unobtainable), but I make no apology for that. They are worth trying to find. Planted as I have suggested, and given *some* maintenance, you will have a garden that is at most times a pleasure to be in and never a burden.

Visit your plants, talk to them, love them – you will have plenty of time to do this if you are not constantly scrambling around on your knees – and you will have a garden that you can actually *enjoy*.

Imagine!

INDEX